GUN
CONTROL
ON TRIAL

BRIAN DOHERTY

GUN
CONTROL
ON TRIAL

INSIDE THE SUPREME COURT BATTLE OVER
THE SECOND AMENDMENT

CATO
INSTITUTE
WASHINGTON, D.C.

Library of Congress Cataloging-in-Publication Data

Doherty, Brian, 1968-
  Gun control on trial : inside the Supreme Court battle over the Second
Amendment / Brian Doherty.
    p. cm.
  Includes bibliographical references and index.
  ISBN 978-1-933995-25-0 (hardback : alk. paper)
    1. Firearms—Law and legislation—United States.   2. Gun control—
United States.   3. United States. Constitution. 2nd Amendment.   4. Firearms—
Law and legislation—United States—Cases.   5. Gun control—United States—
Cases.   6. United States. Supreme Court.   I. Title.

KF3941.D64 2008
344.7305'33—dc22   2008045225

Cover design by Jon Meyers.

Printed in the United States of America.

CATO INSTITUTE
1000 Massachusetts Ave., N.W.
Washington, D.C. 20001
www.cato.org

To my parents, Frank and Helene Doherty, who
taught me freedom and responsibility.

"In America we may reasonably hope that the people will never cease to regard the right of keeping and bearing arms as the surest pledge of their liberty."—St. George Tucker

Contents

ACKNOWLEDGMENTS   xi

INTRODUCTION: *HELLER* MAKES HISTORY   xiii

1. The Roots of the Second Amendment   1

2. The Genesis of *Heller*   23

3. The Politics of Gun Control   43

4. Gun Stories, Gun Culture, and Gun Prejudice   71

5. Guns by Numbers and *Heller*'s Day in Court   85

6. The *Heller* Aftermath   109

SELECTED BIBLIOGRAPHY   117

TABLE OF CASES   119

INDEX   121

Acknowledgments

My thanks go to all those who allowed me to interview them for their valuable insights on the *Heller* case; to the Second Amendment; and to all the tricky and complicated historical, legal, and empirical issues surrounding the case and the debate over guns and gun regulation. My understanding would have been sadly deficient without the generous sharing of insights, information, observations, and stories. Of course, any remaining misunderstandings or errors are entirely my responsibility and not theirs.

Some of them did not wish to be named. The others are here thanked, in alphabetical order: Bob Barr, Alice Marie Beard, Kenn Blanchard, Jeff Bregman, Chris Cox, Richard Feldman, Todd Gaziano, Alan Gottlieb, Martin Green, Alan Gura, Stephen Halbrook, Andrew Hanson, Tracey Ambeau Hanson, David T. Hardy, Gene Healy, Dick Heller, Dennis Henigan, Matt Hughes, Joe Huffman, Gary Kleck, David Kopel, Robert Levy, George Lyon, Joyce Malcolm, Alan Morrison, Clark Neily, Peter Nickles, Tom Palmer, Gillian St. Lawrence, Laurence Tribe, Dane vonBreichenruchardt, and Dave Weigel.

Thanks also to Tim Lynch and David Boaz at the Cato Institute for recruiting me for this project and for all their helpful insights, guidance, and support along the way. Thanks to Cato intern Andre Havrylyshyn, who found needed sources and information with great speed and skill. Thanks to all my colleagues at *Reason* magazine for giving me the time and support necessary to get this book done; to Ivan Osorio and Nick Gillespie for their hospitality during my research visit to the District of Columbia; and to friends who gave needed advice, leads, and support as I researched and wrote this book: Jon Alloway, Tim Cavanaugh, Allison Glock, Tayler Jones, Michael Malice, Cameron McHenry, Alan Ridenour, Stephanie Sailor, Heather Schlegel, and Daniel Browning Smith. Thanks to Noah, Nina, and Adam of Abbot's Habit, home of the best coffee and food on Sunset Boulevard, for allowing me to sit there all day for months writing this book. Special thanks to my wife, Angela Keaton, for putting up with all the usual, and some unusual, difficulties and tensions on the path to getting this book done.

Introduction: *Heller* Makes History

Early on the morning of March 18, 2008, before the sun began to warm the stone plaza in front of the wide, sweeping front steps and regal colonnade of the Supreme Court of the United States, hundreds of people had gathered. They formed a ragged line stretching around to the northern side of the Court's pillared halls.

The crowd bore the long wait standing or sitting on chilly stone, many with nothing but overcoats for pillows or blankets. Still, they were excited, neither aggravated nor bored. The first 50 or so had been there overnight to claim the first-come, first-served chance to sit inside the courthouse's hallowed halls, to see and hear the justices and lawyers spar firsthand. It was worth the trouble. American history would be made there, that day.

That District of Columbia specialty, the professional line-sitter, held some places for those who couldn't wait all night themselves, but who couldn't risk missing the look on Justice Antonin Scalia's face, the tone of Justice John Paul Stevens's voice, as they jousted over a question that had divided both courts and the American people for decades.

Starting at 10:00 a.m. that day, the Supreme Court would hear the oral arguments in *District of Columbia v. Heller*. That case asked the Court to make its first modern-era pronouncement on one of the Bill of Rights' core elements—and greatest sources of controversy and confusion. The crowd was there to hear how the justices would treat the arguments of the lawyers for the District of Columbia— which for 32 years had completely forbidden its citizens to possess usable firearms, even in their homes—and the arguments of the lawyers for Dick Heller—a man who wanted to have a legally registered handgun for personal defense in his home. The case's resolution promised to settle the meaning of America's most contentious constitutional right: the right to possess arms, guns . . . dangerous weapons.

The objects at issue in *Heller* are called many things, some objective and some judgmental. Similarly, Americans hold many opinions, some calm and some emotionally charged, on that right's importance, its propriety, and its very existence. The right in question was officially set in place—or perhaps *not* set in place—in the Second Amendment to the Constitution, the second in what we call our Bill of Rights: "A well regulated Militia, being necessary to the security of a free State, the right of the people to keep and bear Arms, shall not be infringed." That is just 27 words, three commas, six nouns. Yet millions of words of analysis and invective have flowed from it. All that was to come to a head in just over an hour of talk, questioning, and debate.

The crowd outside the Court contained lawyers and law geeks, gun enthusiasts and gun haters, tourists from Texas and law students from Georgetown University—and one toddler I spotted. They were a very white crowd for a city as racially mixed as D.C., and skewed young. They were united in their excitement. They were divided in their hopes and expectations for what the Court would decide.

The crowd was animated, but not manic. Their mostly quiet conversations, knowing nods, and oracular pronouncements about constitutional standards might lead you to underestimate the intensity of the energy, passion, lobbying, activism, lawmaking, and punditry that the topic of gun rights and gun control sparks across America. Even if the crowd wasn't at heart legal and policy wonks eager to bask in the warmth of the hottest political and legal game in town, decorum and dignity would be strongly advised. They were surrounded by a bevy of cops, security, and cameras, who were dogging the shifting groups of protesters and counterprotesters there to play to the media and crowds.

When I strode to the front of the line to chat with the dedicated few who had given up more than a day of their life for their spot, I was quickly shooed away by a cop. If I hadn't earned my position on that plaza between the Court's two stone fountains fair and square, they wanted me to shuffle off: I had no inherent right to take up space in the Supreme Court plaza on such a hectic day.

Those cops and protesters and counterprotesters reminded us that the issue we were there to hear argued was deeply contentious. The Second Amendment debate is intimately entwined with a longlasting, and likely unending, public conversation over the relationship between intimate individual rights to preserve your life and property using the best means available and public attempts to manage the perils that can accompany standing up for your life and dignity in a dangerous world using dangerous weapons.

Embedded in the gun debate, blocking any clear line of sight on what is legally implied by the "right of the people to keep and bear arms," are fears of death and fears of crime, worries about class warfare and worries about political warfare, deep divisions based on self-identity and honor and dueling visions of the proper role of the state and the necessary obligations of the citizen. Each of the dueling sides often sees the other as so mysterious, untrustworthy, and different that meaningful communication seems impossible.

From plaid-clad hunters in the woods to Armani-suited lawyers in penthouse offices, from tweedy academics to cops on the beat, Americans wondered: What exactly does the Second Amendment mean? And what can government, at what level, do or not do because of it?

Inside the Supreme Court we would witness the game-changing colloquy that would hopefully answer those questions. The result would affect—though not settle—policies and emotions that stretch beyond the specifics of the challenge Dick Heller and his lawyers had aimed at D.C.'s gun regulations. Down the line, it would shed light on the fate of every gun regulation in the country, from complete bans on owning certain types of weapons to regulations on where and when legal guns could be sold.

After the session was over—the justices were so interested, so engaged in the back and forth with D.C.'s lawyer, Heller's lawyer, and the U.S. solicitor general that they allowed the hearing to stretch a rare 22 minutes over the allotted 75 minutes—the dueling parties held mini-press conferences between a stone fountain and a pack of a couple of dozen reporters, cameras, and microphones thrust out.

D.C. Mayor Adrian Fenty, head shaven, dapper, and intense, insisted that his city must stand by its 32-year-old attempts to keep guns out of everyone's hands because those policies were making D.C. safer—though it manifestly was not safe. For example, in only one of the years since D.C.'s current gun regulations were passed in 1976 has D.C.'s murder rate been less than in that year; in 10 of those years it was more than *twice* that rate. His chief of police, Cathy Lanier, analogized her city's complete ban on any defensive gun possession with the fact that she had to give up *her* weapon to enter the Court that morning. His acting attorney general, Peter

Nickles, explained patiently that *all* rights are subject to "reasonable regulation," and that whether or not the Court decided that the Second Amendment certified a right that Heller could claim (D.C. did *not* believe it did), D.C.'s ban on handguns was still reasonable and proper.

Plaintiff Heller, with his thin gray hair swept back off his broad forehead and wearing a light tan overcoat, delighted some of his rabid fans in the "what part of 'shall not be infringed' don't you understand?" wing of the gun-rights movement by telling the gathered reporters that "well-armed citizens" make for "a very polite society." While delighting the radicals, it made his lawyers, who wanted to keep their argument rooted in self-defense in the home, cringe a little.

Their press pitches made, both sides had to wait—for months. It took until June 26, the very last day of the 2007–2008 term, for the *Heller* decision to be released. It was written by Justice Scalia.

The Supreme Court, in a 5–4 decision, declared that, yes, the Second Amendment does secure an individual right to keep and bear arms; and yes, the District of Columbia's existing regulations on gun ownership and use—regulations that amount to a complete ban on any usable weapon for self-protection, even in the home—violate that right, and the ban cannot stand. *District of Columbia v. Heller* was over. D.C. lost. Heller won.

It was that simple—and also maddeningly complicated.

The Supreme Court's decision in *Heller* was both an end and a beginning in a political and legal battle that has been waged—with varying degrees of passion and engagement—since the American founding, and even before. Our English heritage of liberty and of government attempts to encroach on that liberty were also implicated in the questions about weapons and militias embedded in the Second Amendment.

The Supreme Court delivered an authoritative answer to one narrow—but vitally important and endlessly contentious—question regarding the Second Amendment. The justices came to that narrow answer by a narrow margin, 5–4. So both the question and the answer are vulnerable to rethinking and adjustment by future courts, if and when one of the many future challenges to gun-control regulations that the *Heller* decision itself emboldened rises back up to the Court.

The *Heller* decision does not, then, settle or even fully address every controversy in the gun-control debate. It only settles the legal question of whether or not the right to possess weapons under the Second Amendment extends to personal self-defense: it does. And *Heller* settles the policy question of whether gun control laws (at least federal ones) can completely nullify a citizen's ability to use weapons for self-defense in the home: they can't.

It is one thing to define the constitutional limits within which any gun regulations must live, as the *Heller* decision did. But within those limits, many questions remain about what sort of gun-control policies are wise, not just constitutional. For example, just because the decision leaves open the question of whether it's constitutional for government to rigorously restrict the right to carry a gun for self-defense *outside* the home doesn't mean that any government ought to do so, if its citizens lives and safety are to be valued.

Before *Heller*, the questions of what right the Second Amendment guaranteed, and what sort of regulations of that right would pass constitutional muster, had been hotly debated for many decades. Contradictory dicta (nonbinding statements in a court opinion that are not essential to the determination of a case) and pronouncements streamed out in law review articles, books, and television chatter from law professors, judges, pundits, and lobbyists.

After studying Scalia's detailed explanation, 67 pages long, of how the Court came to its decision in *Heller*, the layman might find it strange that the debate could have raged so long. How could nimble and learned legal minds have been at such loggerheads for so long over certain elements of the Second Amendment's language and history that seem on their surface obvious and simple? Scalia had to bring to bear the authority and reasoning of the most influential Court in the world to reach such insights as this: the word "keep" in the Second Amendment does indeed mean that Americans can, yes, keep arms in their homes in the everyday sense of that term.

That's one of the fascinating, though often maddening, things about the legal, political, and scientific debate over gun control in America: many seemingly obvious things have been obscured by layers of ill-thought-out legal opinions that have led to reams of paper from legal scholars and activists. All that got piled on the Second Amendment until anything clear about its language and history became dim.

But the Second Amendment is only the top layer of America's gun policy debate. When it comes to guns, many people don't necessarily care what constitutional right might or might not be guaranteed by the amendment. Some people just want to heavily regulate, or even ban, private ownership and use of guns, because they think that is wise public policy. They are willing to obscure what the Second Amendment meant to those who ratified it and to grasp the thinnest line of precedential reasoning to "prove" that there is not, and never was, any such thing as a personal right to own and use weapons for self-defense in the home in America. This legal and historical reasoning is just culture war by other means, wherein seemingly obvious points are adamantly denied and the argument is backed by a long series of learned and erudite footnotes.

What the Supreme Court decided in *Heller* may be narrow in its direct and immediate effect, but it's deep in its implications for the relationship between the government and the American people. It establishes a new shape for the arena in which the legal and political struggle over guns and gun control will be fought. And that fight assuredly continues.

The Second Amendment is part of the founding document of the United States of America. As such, it has been mentioned and considered in many Supreme Court cases. However, *Heller* was the first time the Court fully and unambiguously answered the most basic question about what the amendment means, what right it protects.

The Supreme Court only has to think about what the Constitution means or implies when someone challenges a law for allegedly violating it. For most of our history, few federal laws impinged on citizens' right or ability to own weapons at all. Since the 19th century, many state and local laws did so. But that didn't matter much in terms of the Second Amendment at first. The Bill of Rights was largely believed to restrict actions of the federal government only (at least after the 1833 case *Barron v. Baltimore*). However, in reviewing the history of gun-related legal decisions in chapter 1, I'll show that various state courts and legal scholars always believed the right inherent in the Second Amendment constrains governments at any level, not just the federal.

In 1868, the Fourteenth Amendment was ratified. That amendment was designed to apply to all citizens of all states the privileges, immunities, and right to due process of law inherent in American citizenship. To its framers, this meant that even state and local governments should not be able to violate the core, fundamental rights protected in the Bill of Rights. Even so, in the decades after the Civil War, the Supreme Court never said whether the Second Amendment should be thought to restrict the actions of states or localities, or precisely what rights the amendment did protect. When the Court addressed the Second Amendment after the Fourteenth Amendment was in effect, it stuck to the view that the Second Amendment did not constrict state actions—directly contradicting the clear intentions of the Fourteenth Amendment's ratifiers. And until the National Firearms Act of 1934, very few significant federal laws impacted the right to keep and bear arms anyway.

In the past 50 years, the number and extent of laws regulating the ownership and use of guns grew on the federal, state, and local levels. A previously unknown political constituency arose, one with a great deal of influence—especially on the public. This is what might be called the "gun-control movement," the activists and pressure groups that consider guns a scourge on America—merely accessories to crime and mayhem and tragedy rather than a key part of its cultural heritage and a necessary tool for the vital human right of self-defense. Levels of violence associated with guns rose in the 1960s. Gun control became a hot issue in statehouses and Congress, in newspapers and newsmagazines and legal journals, and in courts at every level *but* the highest.

For decades, the Supreme Court never missed a chance to duck the responsibility of grappling with the Second Amendment, letting stand as their final word on the topic (until *Heller*) the deeply unsatisfying and ambiguous *United States v. Miller* decision in 1939. See chapter 1 for the strange story of *Miller*, the epochal Supreme Court case in which the nongovernment side failed to even file a brief or make a case, and whose main holding has been consistently misinterpreted by lower courts.

But the *Heller* decision, as congenial as it was to those who treasure the right to bear arms, arrives in a nation where that right is circumscribed in many complicated ways, at many different levels—ways too detailed and complicated for any average citizen, and most lawyers, to be fully aware of without dozens or hundreds of hours of research. When I bought my first handgun while researching this book, in California, I was warned I'd better buy a book explaining how to avoid getting stuck in the thicket of confusing state and local laws that constricted such ownership. I'm glad I did. Given the narrow holding in *Heller*, no one can be sure how the right the Court recognized will impact the dizzying array of laws that regulate or restrict the ability to buy, sell, own, store, and use weapons.

The *Heller* case got to the Supreme Court against great odds and from humble beginnings. Its immediate origins were in another federal case, one the Supreme Court declined to take up, decided in 2001 by the U.S. Court of Appeals for the Fifth Circuit. That case was *United States v. Emerson*. It was as significant for Second Amendment jurisprudence as *Heller* in its own way. It was the first case in the modern era in which a federal appeals court declared unequivocally that the Second Amendment did indeed protect an individual right to keep and bear arms.

Why did it take so long for a federal court to decide that the Second Amendment guaranteed a right for an individual to keep and bear arms, given that the words "... the right of the people to keep and bear Arms, shall not be infringed" appear right there in black and white? Well, sit tight. There's an interesting story ahead— and not one you can understand in purely legal terms.

Emerson's holding thrilled gun-rights advocates, even though Emerson, who claimed his right to possess a weapon had been violated, ultimately lost his case. The decision was the culmination of a long, slow growth in the status of and respect for the Second Amendment cultivated in the legal community. That growth took roots in legal scholarship and academia before bearing fruit in the courts.

Legal academics, and most courts, had tended to treat the Second Amendment in the 20th century as if it protected a right, not of individuals to own weapons, but of states to form and arm militias. This was known as the "collective rights interpretation." A more subtle version of it, one which still meant that no one had the right to a personal weapon, is that the amendment protected an individual right but only in the context of membership in an organized state militia. It was this version that was argued for by D.C. in *District of Columbia v. Heller*.

However, in a process that will be explained further in chapter 1, over the past 20 or so years, the more typical view in legal academia has been the one argued for by Heller's lawyers: the Second Amendment indeed protects an individual right. *Emerson* was the first time since the 1939 *Miller* decision that a federal court had explicitly agreed.

While granting that the Second Amendment protected an individual right, the Fifth Circuit declined to say that that right provided any legal protection to Timothy Emerson, deprived of the right to possess a gun because he was under a domestic restraining order. The lower court decision in the case had been more radical in the gun-rights direction. Not only did it declare that the Second Amendment protects an individual right, it also held that that right could not be taken away merely by "a boilerplate order without particularized findings." (The full story of *Emerson* will be told in chapter 1.)

Emerson pleased the gun-rights crowd and angered and frightened those who want the government's power to regulate gun possession and use to be limitless. It also made both proponents and opponents realize that a crack had been hewn in the suffocating granite in which the issue had been encased—at least since the Supreme Court's ill-thought *Miller* decision in 1939. (Most states have their own constitutional provisions regarding the right to bear arms, and those have been treated with much more respect by state courts.)

Something was going to slip through that crack. Some new legal challenge would surely arise to some existing gun control regulation. The Supreme Court faced what is known as a "circuit split" (when at least two different lower federal courts from different districts have made opposing pronouncements) regarding the meaning of the Second Amendment. Thus, the Court was all the more likely to finally stand up to the fusillade of troubles that would accompany a visit to the no man's land of weapons-right jurisprudence.

As the players involved tell it, the idea for something like the *Heller* case occurred to many different people. The short version is this: a small gang of philosophically dedicated lawyers came together, thoughtful libertarians believing that Second Amendment liberties were vital to the American experiment in ordered liberty and that a chance to vindicate them in the highest court in the land was at hand. They decided to craft a solid, clean civil rights case to overturn the most onerous and restrictive set of gun laws in the country. Those laws reigned in the very place where the government created by the Constitution, and hemmed in by the Bill of Rights, resided, along with the members of the Supreme Court who would ultimately settle the matter: Washington, D.C.

A group of lawyers, which included at various times Robert Levy, Clark Neily, Gene Healy, and Alan Gura, found plaintiffs who could present a clear case that they were being denied a vital constitutional right. The plaintiffs were also chosen for their ability to pass muster before the court of public opinion, which is equally vital to any sustainable vindication of Second Amendment rights.

Someone was going to reach the Supreme Court with a challenge to a firearms regulation. Various D.C. public defenders with street-criminal clients who had, generally in addition to other charges, gun possession convictions hanging over their heads, were trying to apply *Emerson's* Second Amendment ruling to knock at least some months off their clients' time. The Second Amendment would suffer if the plaintiff trying to vindicate it were a carjacker or someone who had knocked over a 7-Eleven. Levy thought it quite possible that four mischievous anti-gun rights justices might agree to hear such a case to make sure the Second Amendment had just such a tarnished champion before the Court.

After much searching, Levy's group found six upstanding plaintiffs to join together to launch the case that reached the Supreme Court as *District of Columbia v. Heller*, though it began as *Parker v. District of Columbia*. The original six plaintiffs were a Rainbow Coalition of sorts: two black women, and one gay white male, two straight white males, and one straight white female; otherwise known as a federal bureaucrat, a libertarian think tanker, a lawyer, a community activist and information technology professional, a private security guard, and a real estate investor. None of them was a criminal. All of them had compelling arguments for why D.C.'s gun laws, which made any use of a gun in the home for self-defense impossible, harmed them in a way a court could remedy.

Levy and his team of lawyers filed the case with the U.S. District Court for the District of Columbia on February 10, 2003. The case met initial defeat, then a victory, then more partial defeats. It met unexpected and strange opposition along the way to what some saw as an unexpected and strange victory. In the end, the case vindicated the notion that D.C.'s gun laws violated the constitutional rights of the plaintiffs—and by extension, of all its citizens.

The victory relied on help, coordination, and advice from a wide spectrum of the community dedicated to Americans' civil rights and Second Amendment rights, including law professors, retired generals, police officers, senators, Justice Department officials, and activists for the rights of gays and blacks.

The struggle also involved powerful opposition from an unlikely source: the National Rifle Association, well-known as the most long-standing, powerful, and tenacious warrior for Americans' Second Amendment rights. The NRA thought the *Heller* case was a bad idea and fought to kill it with various strategies, from a copycat case to an attempt to render it moot—until it got to the Supreme Court.

Gun Control on Trial will tell the full story of the *Heller* case, the most dramatic and important Supreme Court case of the 21st century so far: its plaintiffs and lawyers, its trials and tribulations, its setbacks, conflicts, and eventual successful resolution. The *Heller* story stretches back to long before the decision itself—and forward to the future of the political and legal battle over gun control in America. Fully understanding the meaning and importance of this epochal Supreme Court decision takes more than knowing the characters, events, and legal arguments—and resolution—of *Heller* itself. Thus, *Gun Control on Trial* will embed the *Heller* case in the history of the right to self-defense in Western legal and political thinking; in the court decisions, both high and low, that have set and reset, clarified and confused, the meaning of the right to bear arms in American law; in the ideological battles and shifting understanding of legal scholars, politicians, and the American public regarding what the Second Amendment does and doesn't say and mean; and in the history of government attempts to regulate the possession, sale, and use of weapons in America and of the debates and arguments that have raged in arenas from political lobbying to social science around guns and gun rights.

The *Heller* decision loudly reconfigured that debate, but it will not be the final word. Thus, *Gun Control on Trial* will also begin to explore the post-*Heller* world of guns and the law.

The lawyers—and when on his best behavior, the titular client—stressed the narrowness of their intentions in the case and the strict limits of the issue to be decided. But whatever their intentions, *Heller*'s effects will ripple beyond the legally narrow—but philosophically wide—issues decided in the case per se. The debate over the Second Amendment has been so long-lasting and so emotional because it touches on core issues of identity, civic obligation, and the relationship between the citizen and the state. The debate is not over and likely never will be. In telling the *Heller* story in the context of all the complicated legal, historical, and scientific debates about guns in America, *Gun Control on Trial* will provide a primer and map to one of America's most defining and vital public policy debates.

As the lawyers and plaintiffs explained to me, *Heller* was important because it was an opportunity to vindicate a right, but not just the right to own or use guns per se. The case was important because it was a struggle to vindicate the most basic human right at the center of the Western liberal tradition, a right without which all other rights and obligations are meaningless or impossible: the right to defend one's own person, family, loved ones, and property in the manner of one's choice. *District of Columbia v. Heller* is important to American history and Western political history for that reason. That right has been questioned, hemmed in, declared a hazard to civilization. *Gun Control on Trial* will tell the story of the fight for that right.

1. The Roots of the Second Amendment

The Supreme Court decision in *District of Columbia v. Heller* declared that Americans have a right to use weapons for self-defense in their homes. That right is protected by the Second Amendment to the U.S. Constitution, the second of what is known as America's "Bill of Rights."

This declaration shocked, saddened, even "outraged" (as per Chicago's Mayor Richard Daley) many. However, most who objected to this ratification of an individual right to own weapons think of themselves as friends of the Bill of Rights and American liberty. The *New York Times*, for example, champion of the First Amendment, condemned the Court's majority as, in effect, cold-blooded killers, lamenting, "The Supreme Court . . . all but ensured that even more Americans will die senselessly with its wrongheaded and dangerous ruling."

But the principle laid out in *Heller* would have seemed perfectly natural to nearly any American of the founding era. To most, it would have been so obvious that the government can't legitimately disarm a free people that even spelling it out would have seemed bizarre and pointless. That the right existed—even if, say, a Quaker might decline to practice it—was as well understood as any social or political convention could be. The only shock that would have arisen out of the *Heller* decision from an early American patriot would have been amazement that laws such as the ones struck down could have existed for so long without being overthrown.

Indeed, one of the advantages promised by the right to bear arms, which the Second Amendment protects, was that the U.S. government would never dare become tyrannical, since the people as a body would always have superior firepower. Even leading Federalist James Madison, who initially opposed the very idea of a Bill of Rights, promoted this idea. Its power to form a standing army notwithstanding, the federal government, Madison noted in *Federalist* 46, would always be facing "a militia amounting to nearly half a million of citizens with arms in their hands, officered by men chosen from among themselves, fighting for their common liberties." Americans, he said, have "the advantage of being armed," which we "possess over the people of almost every other nation." If Madison, a leading Federalist, openly explained that one of the reasons Anti-Federalists had little reason to fear the new government created by the Constitution was Americans' unaltered right to possess guns, it's hard to see how anyone could deny that that liberty was an understood natural possession of Americans among the people who wrote and ratified the Second Amendment.

Like much about early American legal and political systems, understanding the Second Amendment the way Americans in the founding era understood it requires some background in English history. A proximate ancestor of the Second Amendment is this clause from the English Declaration of Rights of 1689, stating that among the "true, ancient, and indubitable rights" secured by it was "that the Subjects which are Protestant, may have Arms for their Defence suitable to their Condition, and as are allowed by Law."

As the use of the term "ancient and indubitable" shows, the politicians who required William of Orange and Mary to accede to this understanding of their subjects' rights before taking the English throne did not think they were political or ideological innovators. Those who wrote the Declaration of Rights wanted it understood that they were not *creating* the rights enshrined in it. They were merely holding the monarchy to honor such rights—even while accepting some limits "as are allowed by the Law"—after nearly a century in which the right to have arms, in particular, had been threatened and harassed.

In her pathbreaking book *To Keep and Bear Arms: The Origins of an Anglo-American Right*, historian Joyce Malcolm convincingly argued that the English position in regard to weapons could be seen as an *obligation*, not just a right: an obligation to serve as peacemakers in their communities and towns, and to serve the king in defense of the realm, in a nation without professional police forces or armies.

To those who think of gun ownership and use as inherently uncivilized, who believe both personal and communal defense are properly contracted out to a select paid elite class, the scenario of individual responsibility for defense of self and community might well be even more shocking than a "right" to have arms. But when and if a "hue

2

and cry" was heard, the Englishman's duty was to take up his arms and track down the criminals that threatened his town. He also had to do his share to keep watch at the town gates while "sufficiently weaponed" and keep fit with target practice in public spaces set aside in villages.

As Malcolm explains, those obligations to have and use weapons in communal defense grew to be seen as an often onerous and objectionable burden. But regarding the principle at issue in *Heller*— home self-defense—the English were punctilious. Even during times when Catholics were otherwise oppressed (out of fear that they intended to overthrow or subvert the Protestant kingdom), the Papists were still generally allowed to keep weapons sufficient for home defense.

And despite the Declaration of Rights' firm and inspirational language, the English right to arms was certainly not indubitable. A right to weapons was in the Declaration in the first place because it had indeed been violated, and recently. Before the English Civil War that resulted in the deposing and eventual beheading of Charles I, that unfortunate king tried replacing the widespread citizen militia with his own field army. In doing so, he set about confiscating the weapons of some citizen militias. The Rump Parliament of the Cromwell era then began to turn the citizen militia from its traditional role of defense of the realm into a machine to disarm the regime's political enemies.

The restoration of the monarchy in 1661 with Charles II was no restoration of unencumbered British rights, or obligations, relating to weapons. Charles II had some (understandable) mistrust of the Republican-era armies that had been responsible for his father's loss of throne (and head). He relied more on his own select militias than on the full body of the people, banned the import of weapons and weapon parts, legally disarmed tens of thousands of former soldiers of the Cromwell era, and ruled that any two of his deputies could legally initiate a search and seizure of weapons on anyone they arbitrarily decided was a danger to his kingdom. Charles II tried to enforce an early form of gun registration by ordering all gunsmiths in the realm to report all weapons they made and to whom they were sold.

In 1671, Charles II's regime also launched an unprecedented incursion, not merely against specific enemies, but on the general ability of Englishmen to own and use weapons: the Game Act.

3

The act forbade anyone without an estate with a yearly value of at least 100 pounds a year (unless of certain hereditary ranks) "to have or keep for themselves, or any other person or persons, any Guns, Bowes, Greyhounds" or even ferrets. It allowed any single justice of the peace, who could himself be a landowner aggrieved by some illicit weapon owner's poaching, to initiate a search. England had suffered previous regulations of a roughly similar sort, restricting the use of certain weapons in hunting to people of a certain income. Such regulation was more about keeping the lower classes in their place than any careful consideration of rights, political philosophy, or even public safety. Laws meant to protect the aristocracy's game hunting privileges had been common. But in the past, they had taken away only items actually used in poaching. Parliament had never before used game laws as an excuse to disarm the population generally.

Just because a law dictates that a certain class of people are forbidden to have guns doesn't mean those people don't have them—or are successfully punished for having them. (Just ask D.C. Mayor Adrian Fenty.) It is worth remembering that the D.C. government today doesn't know to what extent its gun bans have succeeded in disarming its citizens.

Still, Joyce Malcolm found reason to believe that, although the law was intended to give Charles II an opening to disarm the lower classes and, perhaps more important to him, his political opponents, most English citizens, high or low, managed to navigate those years with their weapons intact.

While the right to arms in our English heritage might not have been truly "ancient and indubitable," it was still a right that the English and English colonists had reason to respect. And their vivid historical experience helped them understand the hazards of allowing it to be readily abrogated.

That guns played a huge and central role in American history, on the frontier and elsewhere, had long been an understood and accepted part of American historiography. That understanding helped cement the idea that the Second Amendment secured a necessary, common, and everyday right for the founding generation. Various colonial governments, including Virginia, Connecticut, and the city of Newport, *required* gun ownership. Georgia for a while required that guns be carried to church, at least by white men.

According to weapons historian Clayton Cramer, author of *Armed America: The Story of How and Why Guns Became as American as Apple Pie,* by the time of the American Revolution, militia statutes in *every* colony required free adult males to be armed.

The idea of an America rooted firmly in a "gun culture" was challenged—successfully, for a while—in a book that could have been very influential on the intellectual atmosphere surrounding *Heller.* Emory University historian Michael Bellesiles issued his book *Arming America: The Origins of a National Gun Culture* in 2000. It was an instant sensation in historical and popular intellectual circles for its iconoclastic demolition of an idea that every schoolchild thought he knew: that America was a country in which, based on our birth in revolution, our frontier heritage, and lately perhaps on pure bloody-minded Clint Eastwood cussedness, guns were a central part of our culture, heritage, and practice. As Joyce Malcolm summed up his message in a review in *Reason* magazine, Bellesiles asserted that guns "were heavily regulated, were owned only by a wealthy few in England, played little role in the conquest of the New World, adorned few colonial mantles, were seldom used for hunting, and were borne by few militiamen and even fewer of their friends and neighbors."

Very much because of the modern political implications of this historical assertion, journalists and most of the history profession warmly embraced Bellesiles's book. It was praised in such citadels of respectable opinion as the *New York Times* and the *Washington Post* and copped the profession's Bancroft Prize for the best work of history of 2000.

Then, instead of becoming a well-forged weapon in the fight against the notion that America was born of a "gun culture," Belle-siles's book turned out to be intellectual fraud in the service of an ideological fantasy. Various scholars took shots at Bellesiles's data and found, among other scholarly sins and errors, that he claimed to have examined probate record data that had been destroyed in a fire nearly a century earlier; claimed that his own notes on the records had been destroyed in a flood; completely miscounted and misrepresented what was in the records in the cases where other scholars *could* check what he allegedly found; and generally, as an independent review board found, featured "egregious misrepresentation" and "falsification." In other words, to overturn centuries of

5

settled understanding—and successfully so, for a couple of years—Bellesiles simply and boldly made things up. (After being exposed, Bellesiles resigned from Emory, and his Bancroft Prize was rescinded.)

The America of the founding era was indeed a place where a gun was a common day-to-day accoutrement of life, and a tool vital for both civic and personal purposes. Young America already had a strong tradition of guns as tools for protection, recreation, rebellion, and food. It was a country fresh out of a revolution in which widespread possession of, and some skill in using, weapons was central to victory. It remembered the indignities and dangers of General Thomas Gage's attempts to disarm the citizens of Boston in 1775.

The United States was a country whose citizens had a right—which the government could not abrogate—to possess arms for their personal use. That should have been unsurprising and obvious. And it was. Still, a complicated history lies behind the Second Amendment and what it meant to its authors and ratifiers. That history is generally ignored by those who want to view gun rights through contemporary lenses, through the needs and expectations of a world where frontiers are mostly gone, hunting is sport not necessity, revolution is considered insane, and the standing army is thought by all respectable opinion to be both necessary and proper for the U.S.'s role in the world.

But English political and legal experience imbued early Americans—who were, thanks to their widespread possession of and well-developed skills in using weapons, themselves freshly ex-Englishmen—with the understanding that personal possession of weapons was necessary. This was both for civic purposes—the common defense of the polity against both external enemies and internal tyranny—and for the personal one of defending the most basic of classical liberal rights: that of self-preservation.

While the District of Columbia, its many *amici* (the term for supporters who file what are known as "amicus briefs" with the Court to support the arguments of a party in the case), and public supporters think this right doesn't really exist, the right of self-defense has long been considered a central—perhaps *the* central—human right in the Western tradition. Various thinkers who significantly shaped early American political and social philosophy, from ancient times to more contemporary ones, venerated that right. Among them were

Aristotle, who *defined* the "polity" as those who bore arms; Cicero, who wrote, "Civilized people are taught by logic, barbarians by necessity, communities by tradition. . . . They learn that they have to defend their own bodies and persons and lives from violence of any and every kind by all the means within their power"; British legal thinker William Blackstone, who praised "the Natural right of resistance and self preservation, when the sanctions of society and laws are found insufficient to restrain the violence of oppression"; and 18th-century French Enlightenment thinker Montesquieu, who noted, "It is unreasonable . . . to oblige a man not to attempt the defense of his own life." Alexander Hamilton himself in *Federalist* 28 wrote of the "original right of self-defense which is paramount to all positive forms of government."

Contributing to the misunderstanding of the amendment's meaning has been the fact that two ideas are jammed into it, reflecting the dual role early Americans saw weapons playing in their life. Weapons were both necessary tools of self-defense *and* tools to meet the civic obligation of communal defense of liberty from both outside foes and their own government. The idea of weapons for personal defense was perfectly normal and understood in colonial times. Various state declarations of rights from the revolutionary era include a right to arms and clearly state the purpose was, in Pennsylvania's example, "for the defense of themselves and the state." Some states did rely explicitly on "common defense" language, but those ideas were commonly mixed in early American ideology, not exclusive. The body of American political minds that ratified the Bill of Rights in 1791 considered inserting the phrase "for the common defense." They made the deliberate choice *not* to explicitly restrict the right to arms that way.

The public discussion about the Second Amendment after it was ratified also indicates that Americans of that era would have been shocked if their ownership of weapons was not largely free of government interference. As Tench Coxe, an influential Federalist intellectual, wrote in a popular pamphlet, whose assertions were utterly uncontroversial at the time, "every . . . terrible implement of the soldier, are the birth-right of an American."

It may have been obvious to both sides of the ratification debate over the Second Amendment what it meant and what right it was meant to protect. However, it *did* take until June 2008 for the highest

7

court in the land to authoritatively state what was so obvious it barely needed to be said by the ratifiers of the Bill of Rights. *Something* made the individual rights conclusion less obvious than it should have been. That *something* was the first 12 words of the amendment, called the preamble. "A well-regulated militia, being necessary for the security of a free people. . . ."

The second clause—the "operative clause"—is so precise, so clear, so sweeping, that to read it out of legal existence, as gun-control believers want to do, requires using the preamble as a smokescreen through which the main clause's clarity is obscured. Even with the first clause blocking the view, Justice Scalia recognized in his *Heller* opinion that an individual right could be clearly discerned by the judicious application of some history, grammar, and common sense. The preamble appears to be giving *the reason* for the Second Amendment. Those who think the preamble preempts the individual right often lean on a canon of statutory construction that states that every word of a statute, or a Constitution, must mean *something*. That's a fair interpretive principle—but it doesn't mean you can interpret the preamble to mean something that makes the clear meaning of the operative clauses fall over dead.

As UCLA law professor Eugene Volokh demonstrated in a much-cited 1998 *New York University Law Review* article, "The Commonplace Second Amendment," state constitutional guarantees typically contained explanatory prefaces that were not meant to restrict the right laid out in the substantive, or operative, part. As *Heller* lawyer Robert Levy liked to say, using an example from George Mason University law professor and Second Amendment scholar Nelson Lund, "Imagine if the First Amendment said, 'A well-educated Electorate, being necessary to self-governance in a free state, the right of the people to keep and read books shall not be infringed.' Surely, no one would suggest that only registered voters (i.e., members of the electorate) would have a right to read."

Second Amendment revisionists have gone beyond overinterpretation of the preamble's power in their sophisticated, or sophistical, attempts to nullify any individual right in the amendment. They also argue that "the people" in "the right of the people" means "the people" as a collective, united in a militia, not any specific individual person. In the wider context of the Bill of Rights and the Constitution, the meaning of the right of the "people" in the Second Amendment should be no different from the meaning in the First or Fourth Amendments. The First Amendment speaks of "the right of the people peaceably to assemble, and to petition the Government for a redress of grievances." The Fourth says that "the right of the people to be secure in their persons, houses, papers, and effects, against unreasonable searches and seizures, shall not be violated." Those rights clearly apply not to any political or military assemblage but to each individual American.

If the framers of the Bill of Rights *had* wanted to distinguish a right that applied only to states and their ability to form militias, they clearly knew how to differentiate between "people" and "states." See, for example, the Tenth Amendment, which says, "The powers not delegated to the United States by the Constitution, nor prohibited by it to the States, are reserved to the States respectively, or to the people."

What is the preamble's purpose, from the individual rights perspective? Two ideas were folded into the Second Amendment: the notion that a militia, and *not* a standing army, was the proper bulwark of the people's liberties, and the notion that the people had a right to possess and carry weapons—for many reasons, *among* which was the maintenance of a citizen militia.

The concept and practice of the militia as the founders understood it—that is, the body of the people in arms, assembled to protect its liberty, even if necessary against its own government—has been driven from American life and law, with the National Guard a desiccated remnant of what was once the core of civic republicanism in America. This is why so many Americans see the Second Amendment as confusing, archaic, and unworthy of consideration today.

The preamble, like the whole amendment, is rooted in America's colonial and English heritage of ideas and practice. The standing army was, to the English, a pox on the free Republic. One of the great advantages of the citizen militia, to the people, is it ensured that king or parliament could not expend the people's fortunes and lives on foreign adventurism. A citizen militia is the ultimate democratic check on foreign policy, ensuring that only defensive wars will be fought.

The Stuart years (Charles I and Charles II) had reminded the English how expensive and tyrannical a standing army loyal only to the king's interests could be; a citizen militia remained the final check on royal ambitions, whether domestic or foreign. When ordered to actions they thought inappropriate, the militia could and did refuse to do them. And the Americans debating the ratification of the Constitution and the Bill of Rights had an immediate experience in their Revolution with the potential tyranny of a standing army loyal only to the government and the liberating possibilities of a militia embodying the citizens' power to decide their own fate.

Those who say the militia clause defines the full meaning of the amendment—that it pertains to granting states' rights to control or arm their organized militias—ignore something important about the Constitution. Article I, Section 8 states that the federal government could make its own decisions with regard to forming the militia and calling it into action. "The Congress shall have Power. . . . To provide for organizing, arming, and disciplining, the Militia, and for governing such Part of them as may be employed in the Service of the United States, reserving to the States respectively, the Appointment of the Officers, and the Authority of training the Militia according to the discipline prescribed by Congress."

Advocates of what has come to be known as the "collective rights" model of Second Amendment interpretation have argued that it was meant to re-establish some sort of state right to control its own militia to balance the federal standing army. But when the first Senate was considering amendments to the Constitution, and it had a chance to consider one that explicitly addressed state power over militias, it was rejected.

If D.C. and its *amici* in the *Heller* case were correct, and the right in the Second Amendment was merely a right to participate in a well-regulated militia, and the militia could be organized and armed—or not—at the whim of the federal government, then the Bill of Rights enshrined a right that the government had the perfect right (and power) to abrogate at will. This, of course, makes the right meaningless—exactly how D.C. wanted it.

The interpretation that has developed since the 1905 Kansas Supreme Court case *Salina v. Blaksley*, reputed to be the first court case to articulate the theory that the right in the Second Amendment applied only to militia membership, would have been foreign to the mentality of its authors and adapters. It's not one easily found in the founding era, or the next century either. The original understanding of the Second Amendment as protecting an individual right dominated the 19th century, in courts, legal scholarship, and politics. As collected ably in Stephen Halbrook's pathbreaking book, *That Every Man Be Armed: The Evolution of a Constitutional Right,* the dominant legal minds of the first half of the 19th century were fully in line with what the lawyers in *Heller* argued: that the Second Amendment protected an individual right and one connected with personal self-defense.

St. George Tucker, a judge and legal commentator, in his 1803 edition of Blackstone's *Commentaries,* notes how the Second Amendment took America beyond the English Declaration of Rights, with its qualifications about "suitable to their Condition, and as are allowed by Law." He wrote: "the right of self-defense is the first law of nature. . . . Whenever . . . the right of the people to keep and bear arms is, under any color or pretext whatsoever, prohibited, liberty, if not already annihilated, is on the brink of destruction."

William Rawle, a storied constitutional commentator of the first half of the 19th century, in the days when the notion that the Bill of Rights did not apply to the states was not yet settled doctrine, wrote of how the prohibition on government action in the operative clause is general. "No clause in the Constitution could by any rule of construction be conceived to give to congress a power to disarm the people. Such a flagitious attempt could only be made by some general pretence by a state legislature. But if in any blind pursuit of inordinate power, either should attempt it, this amendment may be appealed to as a restraint on both."

Joseph Story, himself a Supreme Court justice, interpreted the right in the Second Amendment as not only an individual one, but one that empowers the people united to rebel, as the American colonists did, against their own government if it violated their rights: "The right of the citizens to keep and bear arms has justly been considered, as the palladium of the liberties of the republic; since it offers a strong moral check against usurpation and arbitrary power of the rulers."

A string of state court decisions and legislative actions throughout the pre–Civil War years further shows that the individual rights interpretation of the amendment was dominant, with some allowance for regulation, particularly when it came to the concealed carrying of weapons.

In an 1822 state court decision that rings heroic in the hearts of radical Second Amendment fans, *Bliss v. Commonwealth*, the Kentucky Supreme Court declared that not only was the right as presented in their state constitution individual, it was absolute. (The Kentucky constitution stated that "the right of citizens to bear arms in defense of themselves and the state, shall not be questioned.") Bliss challenged a conviction for violating a concealed weapon statute for carrying about his sword cane. "Whatever restrains," the court wrote, "the full and complete exercise of that right, though not an entire destruction of it, is forbidden by the explicit language of the constitution."

That went a bit far for the time, an era when lots of states passed laws regulating or barring the concealed carrying of handguns (which was thought of, ultimately, as just sort of sneaky and underhanded). Kentucky's legislature openly disagreed with the court decision, and the state constitution was amended so that regulations of concealed weapons of the sort at issue in *Bliss* were permissible.

Other important state cases show what the weapons right meant to America in the 19th century. One, *Simpson v. State,* an 1833 Tennessee case regarding the open carrying of weapons, said that merely carrying weapons did not constitute an illegal action under the common law concept of "affray," an affray being a violent or noisy quarrel that breaches the public peace. In doing so, the court declared that the Tennessee state weapon's right provision, which *did* include the phrase "for their common defense," still meant that "an express power is given and secured to all the free citizens of the State to keep and bear arms for their defense, without any qualification whatever as to their kind or nature."

In the 1846 case *Nunn v. State*, Georgia's Supreme Court relied on the sort of natural rights reasoning that underlay the U.S. Constitution to conclude that the right acknowledged in the Second Amendment is "too dear to be confided to a republican legislature" and thus should not be infringed by government at any level. (The statute at issue in the case, which involved *concealed* weapons, was upheld regardless. And the court, "incorporation" be damned, relied on the federal Second Amendment in declaring that a ban on *open* carry would be "in conflict with the Constitution, and void.")

Similarly, Texas's Supreme Court in the 1859 case *Cockrum v. State* said that "the right of a citizen to bear arms, in lawful defense of himself or the State, is absolute. He does not derive it from state government. . . . A law cannot be passed to infringe upon or impair it, because it is above the law, and independent of the law-making power."

The arguments underlying *Heller* were hardly eccentric in the 19th century. Rather, they were fully in line with how most legal minds interpreted the Second Amendment. But by the 21st century, the individual right interpretation had faded from legal memory in the federal courts. A new era of Supreme Court constitutional interpretation was at stake in *Heller*, not merely how the Court applied an understood doctrine to a specific set of facts.

The Supreme Court had long neglected the Second Amendment, leaving no well-defined path of reliable jurisprudence leading up to *Heller*. Despite the common, tendentious misreading of *United States v. Miller*, the Supreme Court had, up to and including *Miller*, at least shown a tendency to believe that the amendment protected an individual right—even if the Court had never authoritatively held it so in overturning a statute. (How often this case has been misinterpreted is entertainingly and thoroughly explained in a 1996 *Cumberland Law Review* article by Brannon P. Denning, "Can the Simple Cite Be Trusted? Lower Court Interpretations of *United States v. Miller* and the Second Amendment.")

But is that individual right a barrier to restrictions by states or localities? The record there is far more damaging to the gun-rights case. Even after the victory in *Heller*, the answer—for now—is pretty clear: no, it does not. But that doesn't mean the interpretation is correct, just, or irreversible. The adopters of the Fourteenth Amendment were very concerned with how blacks were being unjustly disarmed, both by the law and by terror inflicted by Southern partisans and racists in the wake of the Civil War. Such race-based gun regulations had a long and shameful history in America, with some colonial regulations also disarming blacks specifically (and in some cases making supplying Indians with arms a capital offense).

The man who introduced the Fourteenth Amendment was clear about what he intended it to accomplish. Sen. Jacob Howard (R-MI) announced that the amendment should force the states to respect "the personal rights guaranteed and secured by the first eight amendments to the Constitution; such as freedom of speech and of the press; . . . the right to keep and bear arms."

This understanding as to what rights the Fourteenth Amendment was intended to preserve was well understood at the time, by supporters, opponents, and the general public. Senator Howard's stirring speech of May 23, 1866, introducing the amendment appeared on the front page of the *New York Times* and in many other papers around the country. Surveying the state-level debates about its ratification, as Halbrook did in his 1998 book *Freedmen, the Fourteenth Amendment, and the Right to Bear Arms, 1866–1876,* also buttresses the notion that the original understanding of the amendment was to require states and localities to honor the Bill of Rights. And this definitely included the personal right to keep and bear arms. Various Southern states amended their constitutions after the Fourteenth Amendment passed to reflect that understanding.

Yet, two late 19th-century cases definitely state that the Fourteenth Amendment does *not* apply the Second Amendment to states or localities. The first one arose from a set of terrible circumstances that were depressingly appropriate considering the origins of the Fourteenth Amendment, which was born of a concern for the violent abuse of the rights of freedmen: *United States v. Cruikshank* (1875) concerned the notorious Colfax Massacre, where a Ku Klux Klan leader involved in ongoing warfare over a disputed set of elections in Louisiana in 1872 burned down a courthouse filled with armed blacks on the opposing political team. Cruikshank was convicted of violating the 1870 Enforcement Act, which outlawed conspiring to deprive citizens of their constitutional rights.

The issues involved in *Cruikshank* were complicated, as were the principles expounded in it. *Cruikshank* contains a statement much beloved, and much misconstrued, by modern opponents of gun rights. Ignoring the classic American tradition of natural rights, they have leapt on the statement that "the right . . . of bearing arms for a lawful purpose . . . is not a right granted by the Constitution" to claim that the Supreme Court has clearly stated that the Constitution contains no right to bear arms. And admittedly, the line sounds bad, out of context. But consider the next line: "Neither is it in any manner dependent on that instrument for its existence." That is, the right to bear arms for a lawful purpose is a preexisting natural and civic right. The decision adds that just as the federal government shouldn't prosecute murder, neither should it adjudicate any protection of that right from private citizens, as in *Cruikshank*. That's a task for states and municipalities.

The opinion stated: "The Fourteenth Amendment prohibits a State from depriving any person of life, liberty, or property, without due process of law; but this adds nothing to the rights of one citizen as against another. It simply furnishes an additional guaranty against any encroachment by the State upon the fundamental rights which belong to every citizen as a member of society."

The case is widely reputed to have explicitly stated that the Fourteenth Amendment does not incorporate an obligation on the states to honor the Second Amendment. However, that interpretation isn't entirely clear because the case involved a private action, not a state action. If the decision's reasoning *does* mean that the Second Amendment is explicitly not meant to apply to the states, then *Cruikshank* equally means that the *First* Amendment was not incorporated and thus did not apply to state government actions—a doctrine no one holds to any longer.

An 1886 case, *Presser v. Illinois*, which involved a Second Amendment challenge to a statute barring public parades of armed men without permission, also said the Second Amendment did not apply to the states, ignoring that the Fourteenth Amendment was clearly meant to extend the Bill of Rights to states and localities. The Court's general approach to incorporating the Bill of Rights on the states via the Fourteenth Amendment has changed tremendously in the direction of respecting the amendment's original intention: to extend Bill of Rights' protections to citizens of states against their local and state governments. Although the courts have explicitly stated, since World War II, that most other fundamental rights apply to states and localities, the courts have not yet revisited the hoary and outdated conclusions of *Cruikshank* and *Presser* regarding the Second Amendment.

Indeed, until *Heller*, the courts had shown little interest in revisiting Second Amendment issues. That's why we had to live for 69 years with only 1939's *United States v. Miller* as a guide to Second Amendment jurisprudence from the Supreme Court.

Miller is an unusual case on which to rest an entire edifice of constitutional interpretation. It was, according to one convincing 2007 academic journal article ("The Peculiar Story of *United States v. Miller*" by Brian L. Frye, in the *NYU Journal of Law and Liberty*), essentially a set-up. It was deliberately designed to do what it ended up accomplishing: verify the constitutionality of the 1934 National Firearms Act.

No briefs were filed on the defendants' side, and their appointed lawyer, unable to obtain money from his clients, didn't think it worth his while to go to Washington to actually argue the case. The decision, written by Justice James McReynolds, footnoted cases regarding assertions that the cited cases didn't support. And the *Miller* ruling has been widely interpreted to say something it doesn't clearly say. Yet this was the best the Second Amendment got from the Supreme Court until *Heller*.

The backstory of the plaintiffs in *Miller* is far more colorful and dramatic than the innocuous collection of law-abiding, Constitution-minded citizens in *Heller*. Miller was a professional small-time crook operating around Oklahoma and Arkansas, wheelman for a gang of daring Midwest bank robbers, and a semi-professional ratter-out of other crooks. He ended up dead the same year the decision that immortalized him came down, shot four times, his corpse found on the banks of a dried-up river, his burned-out car on a dirt road in another town.

Miller and partner in crime Frank Layton had, for reasons that never made it into the legal or historical record (but doubtless involved something nefarious), transported a sawed-off shotgun across state lines without having paid the tax required by the recently passed NFA. This was in the days when Congress respected constitutional limits on its power to regulate interstate commerce, and instead of directly regulating or banning guns it thought were over-used by criminals, it imposed a prohibitive tax on them. (It worked: "Tommy guns" largely faded from the American scene, made too expensive by the tax for dealers to want to carry them.)

If Miller and Layton had had their way, this case would never have gotten to the Supreme Court. They initially pled guilty. But Judge Hiram Ragon refused to accept their pleas and assigned them a lawyer. They demurred to the indictment, and Ragon swiftly agreed and tossed out the indictment, declaring that the NFA violated the Second Amendment. While free of the indictment, both small-time crooks went on the lam, uninterested in the constitutional history they were about to inadvertently make.

Judge Ragon was a former congressman, a New Deal stalwart with a strong pro-gun control history. Contemporaneous newspaper accounts, and Frye, assume he overturned the indictment on Miller and Layton deliberately to set up a gimme case, one that he hoped would conclude exactly what he claimed *not* to believe: that the NFA *was* constitutional.

Frye wrote: "Ragon teed up the case. He didn't really think the NFA violated the Second Amendment, and probably colluded with the government. His opinion is peculiar on its face, begging for an appeal. A memorandum disposition is appropriate when deciding a routine case, but not when holding a law facially unconstitutional. And Ragon was the first judge ever to hold a federal law violated the Second Amendment, even disagreeing with another district court which dismissed a Second Amendment challenge to the NFA."

Miller's attorney was too busy to file a brief or show up for oral arguments; who cared, with his clients headed for the hills? He told the Court to just consider the government's side of the case. (The government had to indict Miller and Layton *again* as it neglected to file its appeal on time with the first quashed indictment.) Ragon got his perfect open field to have the NFA declared constitutional, and it was.

Lower courts have carelessly assumed for decades that *Miller* said the right protected by the Second Amendment was not something for any American but had to be connected to militia service. McReynolds's very short bench announcement of the decision said, "We construe the amendment as having relation to military service and we are unable to say that a sawed-off shotgun has any relation to the militia."

The decision went on at greater length. But it did *not* simply declare that Miller had no case since he was not a member of any militia. Rather, the Court admitted that the militia was "all males physically capable of acting in concert for the common defense." What they could not rule on, since no evidence was presented for the argument in the lower court, was whether the sawed-off shotgun at issue "has some reasonable relationship to the preservation or efficiency of a well-regulated militia."

Thus, the *Miller* decision hinged on whether the *weapon* at issue had a militia connection. It did *not* hinge on whether an individual American as a member of the great unorganized militia had a defensible right under the Second Amendment. The decision, although short, tediously explained the importance of the militia and its concomitant *obligations* on the part of men to be armed.

After *Miller*, the Supreme Court was silent in holdings about the Second Amendment for 69 years. But as the 20th-century "collective rights" view slowly conquered various lower courts and federal appeals courts, the Second Amendment itself could be sighted in the interstices of their thinking. It was mentioned in dicta in at least 19 cases post-*Miller*, where it was clearly thought of or at least rhetorically treated like a normal individual right, just like the others in the Bill of Rights. (See David Kopel's 1999 *St. Louis University Public Law Review* article, "The Supreme Court's Thirty-Five *Other* Gun Cases: What the Supreme Court Has Said about the Second Amendment.")

Still, the Second Amendment had become a most unpopular hook on which to hang any legal argument until the bravado of Levy's team led them to file a challenge to D.C.'s laws. As discussed in chapter 3, even the most fervent defenders of weapons-related rights, lawyers supported by the NRA, had been avoiding it. Indeed, the Second Amendment had become just a bunch of curse words to some. In recent attempts to sue a Georgia gun dealer for its alleged responsibility in funneling guns to criminals in New York, Mayor Michael Bloomberg insisted that the Second Amendment not even be mentioned by the defendant, Adventure Outdoors, and the court agreed to his demand.

Levy and his team did not pluck their optimism about a Second Amendment victory out of the blue. A lot had happened in the 1980s and 1990s to make the dawn of the 21st century seem a propitious time for taking a weapons-rights case to the top. Pro-gun-rights scholars had produced decades of work in legal journals, some of it launched and organized by interest groups like the Second Amendment Foundation (which arose from a Young Americans for Freedom–affiliated gun-rights interest group to fill a gap the NRA had not yet filled). That work had shifted how the Second Amendment was viewed—and not only on the political right where the Second Amendment had long been favored. Stephen Halbrook recalled that even mentioning the Second Amendment in his Georgetown Law School days in the 1970s was ill-advised—"no one dared mention it in constitutional law class." And to mention your NRA membership got you openly dismissed as an "idiot from an extremist group."

By 1999, the prominent and liberal Harvard scholar Laurence Tribe had substantially changed his tune on the amendment. In the 1978 edition of his standard text *American Constitutional Law*, he treated the Second Amendment literally as a footnote. By the third revised edition 21 years later, he wrote that the amendment certainly does mean that "the federal government may not disarm individual citizens without some unusually strong justification"; that though the right is "admittedly of uncertain scope," it does encompass a rebuttable presumption that an American can "possess and use firearms in the defense of themselves and their homes."

Other milestones on the move toward a liberal scholarly reappraisal of the Second Amendment included Sanford Levinson's 1989 *Yale Law Review* article "The Embarrassing Second Amendment" and the winning over of liberal academics such as Yale's Akhil Reed Amar and William and Mary's William Van Alstyne to the individual rights side. Second Amendment fans like David T. Hardy and Stephen Halbrook expressed their amazement—and pleasure—watching the very thing they had been working toward since the 1970s, in obscurity and with much derision, actually happen: the rehabilitation and then normalization of the individual rights view of the Second Amendment. Gary Kleck, a sociologist with a specialty in weapons-related research, wrote in his 2001 book, *Armed* (co-written with Don Kates), that of 48 "law review articles published on the Second Amendment in the 1990s, 42 endorsed the individual rights position, and most of the six minority articles were written by employees of gun control advocacy groups."

By 1995, law professor Glenn Harlan Reynolds of the University of Tennessee College of Law could slyly, but accurately, recast the formerly derided individual rights view as the new "standard model" in Second Amendment interpretation. But still, it seemed only the legal scholars knew it, not the federal judges.

The *United States v. Emerson* case finally revived the Second Amendment where it counts (almost) the most: a federal appeals court. It concerned a man, Timothy Emerson, in a bitter divorce proceeding and under a restraining order regarding his wife. Emerson was apparently unaware that federal law prohibited people in his situation from possessing a gun—in his case, a Beretta pistol. Emerson had been said, in court testimony from his wife regarding the restraining order, to have threatened to kill a friend of his wife's, though not to have threatened his wife or daughter. The restraining order, in the language of the Fifth Circuit Court of Appeals decision, "did not include any express finding that Emerson posed a future danger to Sacha or to his daughter Logan." The Beretta that Emerson was arrested for possessing had been in his possession, bought legally from a licensed dealer, prior to the restraining order going into effect.

The initial decision from the U.S. District Court for the Northern District of Texas in *Emerson* was an unalloyed treasure for gun-rights advocates. Judge Sam Cummings not only declared that the Second Amendment protected an individual right, which by that point was unusual enough for federal courts, but also went through rigorous historical, textual, and structural analysis, of the sort that pro–Second Amendment academics had been doing for 30 years—without effect on any federal court.

Judge Cummings concluded that the law Emerson had challenged was "unconstitutional because it allows a state court divorce proceeding, without particularized findings of the threat of future violence, to automatically deprive a citizen of his Second Amendment rights. . . . By criminalizing protected Second Amendment activity based upon a civil state court order with no particularized findings, the statute is over-broad and in direct violation of an individual's Second Amendment rights."

The government appealed to the Fifth Circuit Court of Appeals. There a three-judge panel agreed with Cummings, at least partially, and came down on October 16, 2001, with a 2–1 decision that made the Fifth the first federal circuit to find an individual right in the Second Amendment. The panel ultimately decided, however, that the law stymieing Emerson did not violate that right. The procedure he had to go through, and its reasons for existing, qualified as "limited, narrowly tailored specific exceptions or restrictions for particular cases that are reasonable and not inconsistent with the right of Americans generally to individually keep and bear their private arms as historically understood in this country."

The *Emerson* decision had effects that rippled beyond just the courts. In May 2001, U.S. Attorney General John Ashcroft in a letter to the NRA had already announced that it was his, and the Department of Justice's, belief that the Second Amendment protected an individual right, regardless of whether the Supreme Court had ever explicitly ratified that viewpoint. Then on November 9, 2001, he sent a memo to all U.S. attorneys repeating this statement, praising the appeals court decision in *Emerson* for how it "undertook a scholarly and comprehensive review of the pertinent legal materials and specifically affirmed that the Second Amendment 'protects the right *of individuals*, including those not then actually a member of any militia or engaged in active military service or training, to privately possess and bear their own firearms.'" He repeated and clarified this new dispensation in briefs to the Supreme Court in *Emerson* and *United States v. Haney* (a 2001 Second Amendment challenge to barring civilian possession of newer unregistered machine guns). The Supreme Court, however, declined to take up either case.

This showed how little the DOJ's opinion mattered when it came to most existing gun laws, since DOJ agreed that the lower courts were correct in upholding the gun regulations at issue. Even to a DOJ that believed the Second Amendment protected an individual right, regulations defining both certain suspect classes of people not covered by the right (e.g., those under domestic restraining orders as in *Emerson*) and certain weapons not covered by the right (as in *Haney*) were still acceptable.

Gun-control activists like Dennis Henigan, vice president and legal director of the Brady Center, believe the individual rights model has resurged because of a concerted, nearly conspiratorial, effort on the part of right-wing legal activists to subvert the well-understood and rightly established *Miller* paradigm. In fact, Alan Gottlieb of the Second Amendment Foundation proudly recalled the conferences his group sponsored and the scholars it has supported since the mid-1970s to explore, define, and spread the notion of a Second Amendment that protects an individual right. He's seen the attendance at such conferences grow from 20 or so in the mid-1970s to 300 or more nowadays. So he won't deny that Henigan has a point. A body of intellectuals and activists with similar ideas about the Second Amendment does exist, and they often work in concert. The eventual victory in the *Heller* case represents another example of such a successful intellectual "conspiracy."

Gun rights were advancing in places beyond the courts and the academy. After the damage the assault weapon ban did to the Democratic Party in 1994 (see chapter 3), and a reasonable supposition that gun control worries similarly damaged Al Gore's chances in 2000 in states such as West Virginia and Tennessee, the party was no longer making gun restrictions a major issue either on the federal or state level. (To be sure, various activists in the gun-rights community insist that any apparent reticence on the part of gun controllers of late has been purely tactical and that their overall strategic desire to strongly restrict and maybe eliminate private handgun use remains.)

Laws loosening the restrictions on citizens carrying weapons on their person in public have been sweeping the states in the past two decades. The number of states with "shall issue" standards (objective criteria with little or no bureaucratic discretion) for concealed weapon permits has grown from 8 in 1986 to a de facto 37 today.

That was the legal, political, and social environment in which *Heller* was launched. Taking legal aim at draconian gun regulations was as timely as it had been since the era of stringent gun regulations had begun. Talking like a true lawyer, Levy says of his decision to proceed with a lawsuit against D.C., "The timing was ripe."

2. The Genesis of *Heller*

In the beginning, it wasn't the *Heller* case. It was the *Parker* case, named after original lead plaintiff Shelly Parker. That it reached the Supreme Court as *Heller* rather than *Parker* was just one result of the difficult, tangled, uphill battle, against unexpected foes and barriers, that the case fought from its origin in the imaginations of a handful of lawyers and activists to one of the most controversial and significant Supreme Court decisions in American history.

The *idea* of a lawsuit to challenge D.C.'s gun laws on Second Amendment grounds had many fathers. At the center, however, was Robert Levy. While more than one person talked to him of the benefits and possibilities of such a case, he was the man who recruited a team of lawyers, led the search for plaintiffs, and, most important, agreed to pay for the whole deal. Robert Levy, then a senior fellow in constitutional studies and now chairman at the Cato Institute (a libertarian think tank and publisher of this book) turned the idea into a Supreme Court victory.

Levy recounted the case's genesis to me across the street from Cato's soaring glass-framed tower on Massachusetts Avenue, in a sitting room on the ground floor of the Henley Park Hotel. Levy is compact, bald, and square faced, with prominent ears and an aura of cool, almost menacing competence—he strikes me as the kind of man you would go to to make sure something gets done properly and promptly.

Levy came to the law, and policy, late in life. He made his bones and a sizable fortune in portfolio management and software development, and then at age 50 started law school at George Mason University. Following his libertarian inclinations, he chose not to practice courtroom law but to become a legal policy wonk at the Cato Institute, the largest libertarian policy operation in America. He studied and wrote on antitrust, tort reform, and other recondite legal and constitutional issues.

Levy thinks of himself as a Constitution man, not a gun man. He's not a shooter—and doesn't want to be. His Air Force years were the last time he held a gun. "My interest in the [gun issue] is purely intellectual," he said. "I don't have any personal stake in it. I was and am still a senior fellow in constitutional studies at Cato, so I had all these constitutional issues I looked at occasionally, and this one was overdue to be looked at. Other areas of the Constitution are frankly of more interest [to me]."

Levy recalled being inspired to actually launch the preparation for a Second Amendment challenge in D.C. in June 2002, by two lawyers working at the libertarian legal action group Institute for Justice, on whose board Levy serves. IJ had already taken three cases to the Supreme Court and won two of them. Clark Neily and his colleague Steve Simpson were brainstorming at an IJ happy hour about the possibilities for further legal action after the *Emerson* decision. Then they realized that, hey, they were constitutional civil rights lawyers. This didn't have to remain merely a cocktail party reverie. They could *do it*.

Unlike Cato, IJ does launch lawsuits. It is dedicated to vindicating in court the constitutional rights that more standard civil rights activist groups ignore, generally out of political and ideological prejudice.

Rescuing the most hated, feared, and derided constitutional right of all might have seemed a natural for them. But IJ was not the place from which to launch that rescue operation. To keep its resources and expertise focused, IJ works in only four areas: free speech, economic liberty, school choice, and property rights. Once the case got rolling, Neily's boss at IJ, Chip Mellor, gave him permission to spend some of his spare time on the *Parker* case, but despite Neily's key role on the legal team, it was not officially an IJ case.

Neily, like many Americans, grew up around guns and understood how they should be treated. Guns and shooting were never, though, particular passions for him. Upholders of D.C.'s gun laws, he thinks, don't know some things that he, having grown up in Maine surrounded by hunters, does.

"It's the kind of law only someone who didn't know much about guns would come up with," he tells me. "There really are two very different kinds of people in this country: People who don't have any personal familiarity with guns and treat them like a rattlesnake, think they are literally as dangerous as having a rattlesnake in the house: that that gun will find its way out of the closet and into the

24

children's room and before anyone can do anything about it, it'll do something to them.

"Other people understand a gun is like any other tool: It requires respect. A power saw can be a hell of a dangerous thing; so can a wood-burning stove, a chainsaw, an axe; you just have to treat [dangerous things] with respect."

Just as Neily's involvement did not make it an IJ case, Levy's working at Cato, and the presence of a Cato employee, Tom Palmer, as one of the original six plaintiffs, did not make it a case that "the Cato Institute" was pursuing. While Cato believes in, contributed an amicus brief for, and lent some resources to the case, it does not—as an institution—file lawsuits for policy goals. Besides, said Levy wryly, given that his donations to Cato always far outstripped his salary even when he was a salaried employee (he isn't anymore), it was always misleading to call him a paid employee of the Cato Institute anyway.

Early in the planning for the case, Neily was to be the lead litigator. However, his workload at IJ became a bit overwhelming, and Levy brought Alan Gura on to the case. Neily did all his work pro bono; Gura needed *some* compensation for his troubles but was effectively pro bono as well. Levy said, "His expenses are more than I'm paying him."

Gura, who runs his own small private practice firm, Gura & Possessky, in the D.C. area, wasn't a real gun guy either. He was wearing a grey sweatshirt, sporting boyishly tousled dark hair, and had lively hands when we met for a long interview at a crowded Alexandria, Virginia, coffee house. (It was there, he said, that most of the case's serious work was done.) He does own some guns. (He lives in Virginia, it's perfectly legal.) But he didn't really want to supply a list.

"I've had the questions from reporters: 'Are you a gun enthusiast?' Well, I have a car, but I don't know if that makes me a *car enthusiast*. I have some guns, and I'm very happy that I have them, but. . . . There are people who don't have them, who don't know anybody who has them, and it's foreign to them, even though half of American households have firearms. So they think anyone who has a gun is automatically some sort of gun nut, and I think that's unfortunate. Number one, it's not true. Number two, there's nothing wrong with having guns as a hobby, even though it's not my hobby. I'm not superknowledgable about guns. I have some and I know *something* about them, but I would not hold myself out as an expert. But I think gun ownership is a normal thing. I don't have to be an expert or a hobbyist about guns to have them, like you don't have to be a NASCAR driver to have a car. I just want to avoid getting into detailed discussions about the guns I have because it sounds to people like 'Oh wow, that guy has guns on the brain all the time.' And I confess I don't."

As Neily and Simpson sold Levy on mounting a challenge to D.C.'s gun laws, the idea was floating in the air, post-*Emerson*. Everyone knew that *someone* was going to fight this Second Amendment issue in federal court again. D.C. was clearly the best place to start. One, because D.C. is not technically a state but a federal enclave under direct control of Congress (though it has its own government with a fair amount of home-rule leeway), the litigants could ignore the troublesome question of whether the Second Amendment applied to the states via the Fourteenth Amendment. Two, D.C. had the most ridiculously severe gun laws in the country.

According to D.C. Codes 7-2502.01, 7-2502.02, 7-2507.02, as well as 22-4504 and 22-4515, it was illegal to have a handgun without registering it, and you couldn't register it if you didn't already own it before the law was passed in 1976; it was illegal to have a long gun in your home in any condition other than unloaded and disassembled or trigger-locked; and if you had a registered handgun, even carrying it around your house could get you a year in jail and a $1,000 fine.

Among the people plotting the downfall of D.C.'s gun restrictions was Dane vonBreichenruchardt, a former flight instructor and general interest polymath with a focus on the Constitution. A thick, intense, walrus-mustachioed man, vonBreichenruchardt served throughout the case as friend, adviser, and right-hand man to plaintiff Dick Heller. VonBreichenruchardt remembered trying to sell Bob Levy on a Second Amendment case in D.C. for years before it happened.

He had been running a small nonprofit called the Bill of Rights Foundation, and he was a regular fixture at D.C. area meetings of Constitution-minded legal scholars and think tank activists, especially the Heritage Foundation's Public Interest Legal Group. He and Dick Heller and another roommate, all living together in a house Heller owned in the Kentucky Courts neighborhood near Capitol Hill, daydreamed about bringing down D.C.'s gun regime.

VonBreichenruchardt knew his shoestring operation didn't have the cash to bring such a case to fruition, so he talked up the idea to everyone he could pin down for a minute to listen—including Bob Levy. He recalled Levy always being dismissive about the idea—until Neily and Simpson sold him on its merits. He was surprised when he learned through the grapevine that Levy was really doing it. (Levy said he remembers talking with vonBreichenruchardt about a D.C. Second Amendment challenge but doesn't remember a long history of such conversations.)

In the buildup to the case, Levy recruited another Cato colleague, Gene Healy, who had practiced commercial litigation before returning to the think tank world. Thus, with a cause and a legal team, they only needed clients.

"This issue [was] going to the Supreme Court, so the question was, should it go on behalf of six handpicked, qualified, sympathetic plaintiffs or on behalf of some guy who carjacked somebody or just shot up a McDonald's?" Neily asked.

"We needed people," Levy told me, "who legitimately feared living where they lived without means of protecting themselves. They had to be law-abiding, upstanding citizens who were comfortable with speaking in public. It [was] safer, obviously, to get diversity. We found three women and three men, two African-Americans, four whites, with a vast array of incomes, and ranging from their 20s to early 60s in age."

While one plaintiff in theory is enough to pursue such a case—and in the end only one remained—multiple clients are important not only for the diversity they bring to the case's public image, but also, according to Levy, for protection in the "somewhat unlikely possibility that if you have just one plaintiff and he gets hit by a truck" then it's all over.

With public interest lawsuits, it's perfectly appropriate to literally place newspaper ads looking for clients. Levy and his crew didn't go that far but began talking up the idea in public venues, in magazine articles, speeches, at meetings of their fellow Constitution-minded political types. They were trying to feel out a strategy. Levy wrote a July 22, 2002, op-ed in the *Legal Times* pointing out that dozens of challenges to convictions based on D.C.'s gun laws, mostly by small-time criminals, were already in process.

Levy suggested in that op-ed that gun-rights groups might want to encourage a responsible citizen to volunteer to be arrested for gun possession to establish a test case—a strategy he later abandoned. "It really is taking a chance to have someone break a law, and it's not a great thing in terms of the lawyer/client relationship to be advising a client to go out and become a criminal," he concluded. "That approach should be a last resort, and we did have a different way" to challenge the law.

Gene Healy likes to think of himself as "the Pete Best of the *Heller* case" and gently chided himself in our March 2008 interview at his Cato office for his "claim to fame as the brilliant guy who dropped out of a case that ended up going to the Supreme Court." But he had a book to write on the abuse of executive power and was besides doubtful the case would win. As they were looking for plaintiffs, he regularly searched the Web for interesting gun-related material. He doesn't remember how or why, but he came across a website by a man who called himself, proudly, "Black Man with a Gun." The website at the time, Healy recalled, played a James Brown audio clip when you accessed it.

The "Black Man with a Gun" was Kenn Blanchard, a Maryland man who was both a personal firearms instructor (training law enforcement agents mostly) and occasional NRA representative, doing speaking and outreach about gun laws and gun liberty, especially to the black community. Blanchard was working as a technical writer and recalled becoming acquainted with an information technology worker named Shelly Parker at a company where they were both working. She had asked him about security when she was moving into the District. She asked if he knew any trustworthy firearms instructors. "I said, 'you're looking at one.' From that progressed a relationship of trust and instruction. When I heard the people at Cato were looking for plaintiffs, and [Healy] asked if I knew anybody, thinking they needed an upstanding citizen, recommending Shelly was a no-brainer."

Parker had the potential to be a civil rights icon for a dangerous 21st century, standing up not just for the right to equality, but for the Great Equalizer (as Samuel Colt described the weapons he sold); not just for the right to be treated fairly by some other entity, either the state or a private business, but to have the autonomy to take control of her own life and safety in a polity where that was a very hard thing. She was black, in a community that was around 55 percent black; and that black community would ultimately need to be won over to the idea that the people of D.C. should have the right to keep functioning weapons in their homes.

That, as the Black Man with a Gun knew, could be tricky. The problem is deeply rooted in the history of black families in America, Blanchard thinks. "I found out that [blacks] have been conditioned because of laws with racist roots to them. So mothers who have been matriarchs in African-American families, to keep their men safe, make sure there's no gun in the house. If you want to keep families intact, don't bring a gun into the house! Even though we made it through slavery, made it through the wars, men have become veterans, Big Momma's law still holds. No one *says* they have a gun. All our uncles and grandfathers had shotguns, but there was an unwritten rule we wouldn't talk about it.

"They toe the same line in church: guns are bad." Still, Blanchard is confident from the candid reactions he gets when he speaks to black groups, at intimate gatherings such as fraternity meetings and Tupperware parties, once they decide he's for real, that a lot of quiet civil disobedience to D.C.'s gun laws is out there, of the sort that won't show up in any official statistics.

Parker had a dramatic story of the type that should make everyone this side of gun-control proponent Rosie O'Donnell want to send her an out-of-state mail-order handgun.

In February 2002, Parker, a former nurse now working in software design, moved to a neighborhood on the northeastern edge of Capitol Hill, rife with tenacious young drug gangs. She wanted her neighborhood to be a safer and more comfortable place for law-abiding citizens who didn't want to create problems for others. She made a nuisance of herself to local drug dealers, walking the streets wearing an orange hat as a one-woman citizen patrol, calling cops when she saw illegal activity, and installing a security camera for her yard. By June, her car window had been broken, her security camera had been stolen, and a drug gang lookout rammed a car into her back fence. When the first press about the case hit, one particularly tenacious young drug dealer, physically imposing at over seven feet tall, shook her gate angrily one night shouting, "Bitch, I'll kill you. I live on this block, too."

Having a client with a story like Parker's was good for the case, according to Gura. "I do believe it influences the way the press sees the case. It's good that it not be just a bunch of political activists, but real people with real problems. Civil rights law is about individuals who have real-life, not abstract, concerns that need to be addressed."

Parker's story is harrowing, and it's hard to imagine one that could make the disinterested more sympathetic with the notion that innocent people often need dangerous weapons to defend themselves. But, I asked Levy, aren't judges supposed to rely more on abstract principles in cases like these? Whatever the story, either the Constitution guarantees a right or it doesn't.

"Certainly one would hope [the plaintiff's story] would have no effect on the judges' view of what the Second Amendment means, and I'm not prepared to say it would have," he said. "But it does have an effect in the court of public opinion. If it's the usual suspects, the NRA, the Second Amendment Foundation, [pursuing the case] the reaction is, 'This is the gun rights groups doing what they always do.' But if it's six citizens fearing for their lives, whose stories show they could be injured in D.C., it takes on a whole different complexion, and I think the media reacts to that."

Levy and Healy didn't have to look far to find another client: working in an office upstairs was Tom Palmer, then a senior editor at Cato, now a Cato vice president, with expertise in spreading classical liberal ideas overseas (including stints in the 1980s smuggling freedom literature and copiers behind the old Iron Curtain). He grew up around guns, like many Americans—and also *unlike* many Americans.

"I know people who don't understand why anyone would have a gun. They don't have guns, they didn't grow up with them, and they assume people who did must be some sort of primitive barbarians. This just means they have a total disjunct with a huge segment of the American population. These are not death blasters from space! These are tools," Palmer told me, dapper in a black suit with thin grey stripes and a carefully placed scarlet handkerchief, over lunch at the Henley Park next to Cato. "Dangerous tools, like a car, a truck, or a knife are dangerous tools." He noted that even among the high-level donors at Cato, "they intellectually agree with [weapons rights] strongly, but they are not in the group of people who are as passionate about it. It's not implicated in their day-to-day lives or lifestyles.

"But guns are a very important rite of passage for many millions of Americans, very few of whom have any criminal backgrounds or propensity. It doesn't mean you're some kind of gun nut as you'd read in the media, who are unsympathetic to this way of life. They'll pick some person with 69 guns who says 'I love my guns, every one has a name, this one's Betsy, this one's Melinda, of course I sleep with them.' That's the image people have, but it doesn't correspond to the experience with firearms of most people who have them."

Like Shelly Parker, Palmer knew first-hand how a gun could make his life more secure. Unlike Parker, Palmer already had the experience of rescuing himself from a hazardous situation with the judicious use of a personal weapon. It happened in California over a decade ago. He told the story freely, since the statute of limitations, he figured, is up. He and a friend were walking around one evening when a gang of young men—late teens, early 20s—began harassing them, shouting "'faggots' and 'queers' and so on. They followed us, uttering really credible threats. Two stuck in my mind: 'We're gonna kill you'—it's hard to parse that in any nonthreatening way. And the second gave additional weight to their claims: 'They'll never find your bodies.' This was not just some hooting or catcalls. This was very, very serious.

"I told my friend to run. It was late summer dusk, and I got to a streetlight and turned around and pointed my gun [a 9mm handgun] at them. It wasn't like in movies, no heroic moment or anything like that. But they stopped, and the lead one who had been calling the murder threats was just focused on it. If you've ever had a gun pointed at you, it looks like a cannon, like a gigantic huge hole pointing at you.

"I said, 'If you come closer, I'll kill you,' and that focused him. What was interesting was, there was a handgun initiative on the ballot then, and the first thing out of his mouth was: 'Have you got a permit for that?' I just said, 'You just back up to the other side of the street and go the other way.' And that's exactly what they did. It was a nonmurder and consequently a nonstory. It wasn't in the paper. There wasn't a police report. It was captured in no statistical analysis."

The *Heller* plaintiffs' claims were narrowly about self-defense in the home. Palmer's experience, with its implied lessons about the benefits of public carrying, wasn't *directly* relevant—though certainly people involved in *Heller* as both clients and lawyers believe that public carry should be legal in D.C., at least eventually. But Palmer's story further cemented the idea that, for many people, the desire to own a gun comes not from ideology, or mania, or fantasy, but from direct personal experience.

In early meetings about the case, dozens of potential clients passed through. Many were passed by, for many different reasons. Maybe they weren't sufficiently on message, maybe they weren't sympathetic enough, maybe they didn't meet the diversity mix, maybe their interest in having a gun seemed a little *too* intense. Some people they interviewed got dropped, Neily said, because they "get so wrapped up in their own experience they can't see the world through any other lens. It becomes a personal battle between them and some perceived empire of evil, and that's not a good person [for the case]."

Levy and his team eventually settled on six with which to officially launch the case. Parker had her experience of being actively threatened by violent criminals, and Palmer knew in his bones that having a gun on him may well have saved his life. But while those experiences were certainly good for the overall mix of stories and motives, the lawyers didn't need victims. They were not looking for people who approached the case wanting vengeance on crime, either experienced or perceived. In the early days of the case, Healy recalled talking to clients about the best ways to present their case to the press: "We don't want anyone saying 'I'm really angry I'm not allowed to own a gun.'"

Unlike most of the other plaintiffs, George Lyon, a communications lawyer, is what most would call a *gun person*, if not a "gun nut." Growing up in Richmond, his mother wouldn't even let him own a BB gun. Guns, however, were common in his neighborhood.

"Everybody's daddy had a revolver in the dresser drawer," he recalled. "And I don't recall any accidental shootings." Lyon still remembers with disdain the "idiot scoutmaster" who thought it was funny to occasionally aim and pull the trigger on an unloaded shotgun—a violation of one of the four basic gun-safety rules. They are, in my own formulation, (1) treat every gun as if it is loaded; (2) don't point a gun at anything you aren't willing to shoot; (3) keep your finger off the trigger until ready to shoot; (4) and be sure of what you are aiming at and everything that will be in the path of the bullet.

During our interview in his Kalorama Triangle townhouse, Lyon cheerfully demonstrated some lessons from gun-safety courses he has taken, including the art of "clearing the room." By watching him edge his body, turned sideways with pistol (fake plastic training weapon, D.C. city officials!) forward, out of the kitchen and into the dining room, I could see how small handguns made better defensive weapons for the home than longer, bulkier, more awkward long guns.

Lyon, a precise owlish man who obviously finds the topic of guns and gun laws not only fascinating intellectually (though often exasperating), but also fun, is a disgruntled Republican with libertarian leanings. He has had his mind on the legalities and perils of gun ownership for some time. He once lived with a lady who brought in guns she had owned legally in Virginia and kept them in D.C. on the sly. (The statute of limitations on the crime is past, Lyon said.) Cleaning workers stole the weapons.

It occurred to him that reporting it to the police was tantamount to confessing to a crime, and as a lawyer he was loath to do it. He consulted a friend who had been "high up in the Clinton Justice Department" who told him: "Anything you do will make the situation worse. They won't give you immunity, and they will prosecute if you admit to a [handgun law] violation."

Lyon hasn't had much direct experience with crime. His neighborhood, in the daylight on a Sunday morning when I visited him, was as calm and quietly lovely as you'll find in D.C., with well-tended lawns behind wrought metal gates and in front of attractively painted rowhouses. But it's by no means idyllic. A woman down the block, a congressional aide, was murdered by home intruders shortly after Lyon moved to the neighborhood in 1994.

After *Emerson*, the promise of a lawsuit aimed at D.C.'s gun laws had occurred to Lyon as well. He recalled a meeting with Stephen Halbrook (the Second Amendment scholar and lawyer who works with the NRA). Halbrook was skeptical that the Court would even take a Second Amendment case, much less decide it their way. He told Lyon the ultimate decision from the NRA as to backing such a case would come from its executive vice president, Wayne LaPierre. Lyon never heard from them again. So when he heard from an ex-girlfriend that Levy and his crew were beating the bushes for clients, he was excited, and he was in.

Lyon is a registered owner of long guns in D.C., a shotgun and a rifle. The process took two and a half months, he recalled. "I had to get fingerprinted, have photographs made, had to go to the police station three times—once to pick up forms. They won't mail them, and they were not available online. They try to make it as hard as possible. I sat down there for two and a half hours waiting for them to open up the gun-control office. It was supposed to be open at 8:00 but didn't open 'til 10:30. I sat with a cop who'd been up all night on shift waiting to trace a firearm, and we talked. He said, 'Look, I agree with you guys. We know who the bad guys are.'" (Two D.C. police chiefs have publicly disagreed with the city's gun ban.)

Lyon had to bring his weapons down to the station in the registration process. "That created a degree of anxiety. First thing I did was I called the day before and said, 'I understand I gotta come down there—you guys are not gonna draw down on me as I walk in with a shotgun?'" He brought his Mossberg pump action shotgun in disassembled and boxed. He was escorted to the gun-control office by an officer, stacked his forms with his photographs and fingerprints. Then "I had to wait 65–70 days for absolutely no reason. In Virginia they perform an instant background check. There's no reason for two months of time other than just for a legal hassle."

And, the language of D.C. Code 7-2507.02 makes all that rigmarole Lyon went through pointless. Unless you are using it in your place of business, or for some (unspecified, and more or less nonexistent in the District) "lawful recreational purpose," the gun must be rendered useless through being "unloaded and disassembled or bound by a triggerlock or similar device."

As the law requires, Lyon's weapons, legally registered and owned, are not ready to be used at the short—sometimes split-second—notice that a home intruder might provide. The trigger-lock requirements are "certainly an inhibiting factor," Lyon says. "This is a real life experience: Last Thursday night at three in the morning I was awoken by a burglar alarm going off. Had I had a handgun I would have grabbed it and cleared the house with the handgun. Instead I came down here and cut the alarm off, determined what sensor was activated, grabbed the telescoping baton and cleared the house with that. The reason I did that was because of the awkwardness of grabbing the shotgun, unlocking it, loading it, and trying to clear the house with the long weapon.

"By the way, on that burglar alarm call, I had cleared the house and walked the dog before an officer rolled up about 25 minutes later. In that time, if there [had] been someone here with a deadly weapon intent on destruction, all the police would have done is draw a chalk line. And I don't fault the officer who came. She was very nice. We inspected a window lock that was broken and we both agreed it was the wind and not someone trying to break in. The nearest police station is at 17th and U Street, about eight blocks away."

Lyon wanted it understood that keeping weapons in the home is a grim responsibility for someone who cares about his own and his loved one's safety—not a lark, not something to relish. He has been through weapons training with a pro. He knows facing the reality—even if only in role-playing—of using a gun in a conflict with another human being is harrowing.

"There's absolutely nothing good that happens from pulling the trigger of a weapon to defend yourself," he said evenly, "except that you might live or be able to save someone else who's innocent. The last thing you want to do is use your weapon for self-defense. But if you don't have it, then you could die or someone you love could die."

Not all the plaintiffs wanted a handgun, that forbidden fruit which was completely banned in D.C. unless you possessed it prior to the law's passage in 1976 (see chapter 3). Technically, the illegality worked this way: you couldn't legally possess a pistol or handgun unless it was registered. And you couldn't register one if you hadn't owned it in D.C. before the law went into effect.

Long guns—rifles or shotguns—*can* be registered in D.C., as Lyon did. And the business and recreation exceptions show that the D.C. City Council knew full well how to codify exceptions to its rule. The law, on its face, is clear: *Never* can a citizen of D.C. legally load and use his or her long gun, registered or not, in legitimate self-defense.

Plaintiff Gillian St. Lawrence is more comfortable with a long gun than a pistol. She owns one and has it in her Georgetown neighborhood row house. She'd be even more comfortable if it were legal to *use it* in her home when she was in danger.

St. Lawrence, a lovely, earnest, well-composed young blonde woman who posed proudly with her 12-gauge shotgun over her shoulder in a *Washingtonian* magazine story on the case, got involved after she ran into Neily at a legal conference she attended with her husband, then a Georgetown University law student, now a lawyer. She volunteered herself as a potential client.

She was raised an Army brat in multiple homes in multiple cities but has lived in D.C. her entire adult life. She received a bachelor's degree and a law degree at Georgetown University. Sometimes she takes her long guns—gingerly, wondering what would happen if she had to explain to an officer who pulled her over for a traffic offense why she had a shotgun in her trunk—to Blue Ridge Arsenal in Chantilly, Virginia, to keep herself well-honed in her shooting skills.

The transport rules are strict; she has to be going directly to or from the range to have her weapon in her car. "You can't stop at the grocery store on the way back." She worries what the neighbors think as she walks from car to house with her gun case. "I hope people think it's a violin case, because these people will freak out and call the police. None of these people have shotguns, and they probably don't even know you are allowed to."

Georgetown is reputedly one of D.C.'s tonier and safer neighborhoods. "A lot of people would say, 'Oh, you don't need to defend yourself there'—which is not true, because lots of people break into houses here because they know there's something to steal." She told me of drive-up muggings at the commercial strip a few blocks from her home, groups of criminals approaching groups of drunken college students to snatch iPods, wallets, and cell phones. Even in "safe" Georgetown she has had lunatics banging on her front door at 4:00 in the morning, and mysterious men on her roof who claimed to be workmen "mistakenly" at the wrong address.

Like Lyon, also the owner of a legally registered shotgun, St. Lawrence has spent a lot of time at D.C.'s old gun-control office. She ran into a cop there once, there to turn in a confiscated gun he might have gotten off some ignorant legal owner of a weapon in Maryland or Virginia who mistakenly drove into D.C. with the weapon. He told her that she'd better hope she never uses "that thing" because the city would go after her with everything it had, including trying to take her property. She should "get a big dog" instead of trying to play with dangerous weapons, she was told.

How patronizing, she thought. St. Lawrence has run into sexism on both sides of the issue, from men who seem to assume that she's incapable of defending herself skillfully with a gun to women who think that self-defense is simply too terrible a responsibility. Don't we civilized people have *police officers* to do that for us?

St. Lawrence's message to her fellow women is this: "Yes, you have to deal with the unpleasant fact that someone might break into your house and want to kill you with a gun. So you need to figure out how to defend yourself and get over this irrational fear. But to some women who are just all about their emotions, guns are scary and guns are bad, and they all should be banned. And if we ban them, we won't have to worry anymore because no one will have them. I'm sometimes embarrassed to be of the same gender."

The case's third female plaintiff was Tracey Ambeau Hanson, a federal employee with the Department of Agriculture, a black woman in a mostly black neighborhood near D.C.'s Union Station. It's a neighborhood with few nuclear families, mostly middle-aged professionals with no kids in the household. She's married to another federal employee, Andrew Hanson, who works at the Environmental Protection Agency and who first came to Washington in 1985 as a staffer for Sen. Charles Grassley (R-IA).

Tracey Hanson found out about the case through her husband, who is more actively interested in guns and gun politics than she is. Andrew learned about it from a chance encounter with an NRA official in a sporting goods store parking lot in Virginia. Word in the gun-rights community was spreading about a need for plaintiffs in D.C. for a lawsuit. Andrew looked into it and contacted Levy; in the end Tracey, a black woman, made a more valuable addition to the plaintiff mix than Andrew, a white man.

Andrew Hanson picked me up from the U Street/Cardozo Metro station, on the edge of a neighborhood which, like many in D.C., seems perfectly unmenacing in the day but can be more dangerous than a surface look would indicate. I'm a journalist and think tanker; I'm not well-versed in what are thought of as the rougher neighborhoods of D.C. I did most of my work in the day, in sunny neighborhoods. Things always seemed relatively clean, orderly, and civilized. Most of the time, they are. But sometimes they're not. While I was doing interviews and research for this book, a young policy analyst named Brian Beutler, close friend to many friends of mine, was shot on the street in D.C.'s hipster Adams Morgan neighborhood. And Katharine Weymouth, the new publisher of the *Washington Post*, granddaughter of the illustrious Katherine Graham, was mugged at gunpoint near a *Post* reporter's home. If we are to be responsible for our own lives, we need some insurance for unexpected, rare (but not nearly rare enough), grim circumstances.

The Hansons' block looks, in the day, quite pleasant: orderly, well-maintained old brick rowhouses. Out of context, I wouldn't think it was the sort of neighborhood that would inculcate anxiety. As we started the interview, in their well-appointed dining room, local firefighters were finishing a walkthrough inspecting their fire alarms. It felt like walking the line between quaintly civic and big-brotherish; but nothing about the neighborhood, to this stranger, felt *off* or dangerous. The Hansons' home is tastefully decorated, roomy, comfortable, and feels safe.

But as we chatted, the two of them—in that charming, married-couple fashion of buttressing, amending, and arguing gently with each other's memories—related, casually, the shifting borders of various drug gang territories in the blocks around them. They debated the details of the shootings and the gunmen—gun *boys*—dashing down the alleys behind their rowhouse. And they discussed which dogs got killed when the old ladies walking their dogs got caught in drug gang crossfire.

Andrew grew up in Iowa, Tracey in Louisiana. Both were now federal employees in a city (mostly) legally gunless. But both grew up in worlds where families could and did have guns—and those guns weren't trigger-locked and stored away from ammo. In their experience, no one seemed to hurt or kill themselves or others with guns.

Andrew is an NRA member and talked the dedicated gun-rights-defender line all the way; Tracey makes sure I knew that she does *not* believe concealed carry in D.C. right now would be a good idea. They do own properly registered long guns. They are not in any hurry to show them off, to me or any other reporter who might broadcast that image. Andrew, for his part, thought that a *Washingtonian* feature on the case might have been a time for him and his wife to pose "American Gothic" style—the stoic, symbolic American couple, with rifle instead of pitchfork. Tracey nixed that idea.

Even in a neighborhood more dangerous than most Americans live in, Tracey herself has never felt quite *menaced*. She gently complained about a *Washington Post* reporter who tried to squeeze a Parker-esque personal experience out of her. "She hoped I'd have [some story of threatened violence]. Do you think I'd have that because I'm black? Sorry! My life may be kind of boring to some of you. She was trying to get a story that didn't exist." "The story that existed," Andrew said, "is we care about and believe in the Constitution. But that wasn't very interesting to her. No hook."

Their message was clear as Andrew and I walked out into a gentle spring day on their sunny street. Once we were back in his car, Andrew casually directed my attention to the black teen in a wheelchair on a stoop, his eyes straight forward, face expressionless, the warm afternoon sun on his bare arms. He was paralyzed, Andrew told me, in a shooting. The young man knows who shot him, but won't testify.

That kind of detail, you can read how you want to read it. You might be sad and disgusted about the guns that diminished that young man's life, or you might realize that human society can be dangerous, that guns exist and are not going to disappear, and that to deny yourself a fit tool for dealing with the world's dangers might just be irresponsible.

Dick Heller became the most important of the original six—if only because he was the only plaintiff left by the time the case reached the Supreme Court. Even so, he was somewhat the odd man out. As five of the six plaintiffs explained to me, it's not like the plaintiffs became attached at the hip. They enjoyed cordial and professional relations, mostly, but no real palling around based on their mutual interest in armed self-defense or their mutual fate in being the parties responsible for one of the country's more portentous legal cases. Oh, they'd meet at least a couple of times a year to get briefed by their lawyers on the latest twists and turns in a case that ended up winding through the courts a lot longer than they expected. And they might all get together for pizza then. In civil rights cases, once things get rolling, it's pretty much all about the lawyers.

But Dick Heller, as many involved with the case would quietly admit without wanting to stress it too much, was perhaps the least favorite among the original six to be the poster boy for the case. He was the most like a clichéd vision of the sort of person obsessed with his gun rights. As one prominent figure in the case told me, they couldn't always be confident Heller would stay on message— and the message was *not* supposed to be, "I want guns in case the government starts getting on my nerves."

Heller thinks a lot about the government and all the different ways he believes it overshoots its constitutional bounds. His ideological comrade, former roommate, and handler of sorts, Dane vonBreichenruchardt, is someone he likes to have with him when he talks to the press. Together they planned ways to bring America closer to its constitutional roots.

The best hook about Heller for the press was his day job: a trained and licensed special police officer for the District. He even carried a gun in a federal office building where he'd sometimes see Supreme Court justices and staff, the Thurgood Marshall Federal Judicial Center. Yet, at the end of the day, he had to—"like Barney Fife," vonBreichenruchardt marveled—turn in his gun and bullets and go home, defenseless.

That fact made a great public relations hook for the *Heller* story, as everyone involved recognized. The city couldn't maintain that it's inherently unsafe or problematic that this man, Dick Heller, possesses or handles a weapon. He does it every day; it's his job. And he's deputized to do so by the city itself, background checks and all, though he is technically employed by a private firm—a firm, he told me, that isn't interested in being associated publicly with his case.

Gun rights aren't all Heller and vonBreichenruchardt care about, not even close. But gun rights were, Heller recalled, the reason they launched a small nonprofit called the Bill of Rights Foundation that vonBreichenruchardt managed day to day, trying to influence government and forge left-right alliances on a wide range of constitutional issues, from privacy to the Second Amendment.

During our first interview in a meeting room above a Capitol Hill Starbucks, vonBreichenruchardt handed me an old news clip about him and a plan he had back in the 1970s for a new, improved method to propel bullets from guns, without brass casings. VonBreichenruchardt showed up a good half hour before Heller and did well more than half the talking even when they were both there.

VonBreichenruchardt was a tenant and roommate of Heller's in the 1990s and helped him get thinking about the Constitution. The two of them collaborated in the 1990s trying to get involved in trade missions to newly liberated Eastern Europe. Their first attempt at activism in the weapons-rights world came when they made an aborted attempt to put together a defense fund for D.C. resident

Adrian Plesha, convicted in 1997 on gun possession charges after shooting a burglar—in the back.

VonBreichenruchardt said that he and Heller were freshly afire about striking a fatal blow to D.C.'s gun laws as soon as they heard about *Emerson*. Hallelujah! After decades of being buried in the courts, the Second Amendment was on its feet again, crawling out of the grave in which years of thoughtless reliance on the half-understood *Miller* decision had left it. He remembered haranguing Levy about it for months, thinking he was only a Cato wonk, not realizing Levy might have the money to himself fund such an effort—something vonBreichenruchardt's shoestring Bill of Rights Foundation could never do.

Heller certainly thought he'd be an effective representative for the case. He lived across the street from the Kentucky Courts public housing projects. "Across the street from my front door every night for a month there—until this guy got killed or jailed—he'd fire a gun right at 2:00 a.m. to signal the end of the drug trade for the day. First time I fell off my bed. Then I'd say to myself, my house is brick, and I'm under a level of brick on the second floor, I'm probably safe, and go back to sleep. That's the neighborhood I lived in, that insanity."

As he recalled, those were the days when kick-and-enter robberies were popular among the drug trade. "That happened next door; the girl next door got a gun stuck in her face." If they were from the neighborhood, the crooks might "know everyone in the household is 60 years old, so [they would] just kick in the door and clean out the place."

While that was going on, Heller believes, "every citizen concerned about their safety should have been thinking, gee, they're coming in with guns killing people, we should be able to defend ourselves. But that was my neighborhood, and a description of our culture at the time."

Ideally, a man like Heller, faced with such circumstances, could choose a personal solution, in line with the ancient and natural imperative of self-preservation and self-defense. Unfortunately, D.C. had chosen to restrict him and the rest of its citizens. His solution could not be personal; it had to be political. Politics had been hemming in the right to protect oneself with the best available tools in America for a long time before D.C. decided to ban functional weapons. The road to *Heller* had been long.

3. The Politics of Gun Control

It was a long, unplanned journey from the days when the state of Virginia insisted by law that its male citizens carry arms to courts and church to the day that D.C. could arrest an armed security guard for having one in his home.

Severe state and local gun restrictions began popping up in the 20th century. In 1902, for example, South Carolina banned all pistol sales to civilians. In 1911, New York City passed the Sullivan Act in a wave of anti-immigrant fervor, giving police officials a weapon to ensure the "wrong element"—like Southern and Eastern Europeans—couldn't walk around armed. The law prohibited carrying concealed weapons without a permit, a permit issued at the discretion of city officials. Nowadays, in New York officials' eyes, nearly everyone who isn't a celebrity, politician, or media magnate is deemed unworthy to carry such means of self-defense.

Federal gun regulation began in earnest with the 1934 National Firearms Act. It applied only to certain classes of firearms, mostly shotguns with less than an 18-inch barrel, rifles with less than a 16-inch barrel, and machine guns. The act established licensing of dealers and registration of weapons for those classes. A large tax ($200, in 1934 dollars) on every affected weapon when manufactured or sold made the weapons at issue so prohibitively expensive it killed a lively civilian market in them. This was essentially gun control disguised as a revenue act; it was the law that triggered the *Miller* case (see chapter 1).

A follow-up Federal Firearms Act in 1937 extended some mild, rarely enforced, restrictions on people selling all sorts of firearms in interstate commerce (this was back when the "interstate" distinction was still occasionally meaningful to Congress). The NRA was instrumental in drafting the law, which ended up, to gun controllers' chagrin, mostly toothless.

The next two decades were quiet on the gun-control front. The 1960s gave many Americans reason to fear the gun, given the major political assassinations of two Kennedys and Martin Luther King Jr. and a rising spate of domestic urban violence. The violent crime index more than doubled from 1960 to 1970, from 159.6 to 361.0 incidents per 100,000 population.

In that atmosphere, the Gun Control Act of 1968 was enacted. The bill had been percolating in various forms for most of the decade but gained new life after the assassination of Sen. Robert Kennedy. Attempts to include national licensing and registration for individual owners made some headway, and had the Johnson administration's support, but ultimately failed.

Complicated and detailed, like all modern legislation, the major elements of the Gun Control Act included licensing for gun dealers, manufacturers, or importers. It created categories of people to whom licensed dealers could not sell, including nonresidents of the dealer's state (except under certain special circumstances), felons, minors, fugitives, users of illegal drugs, and those who have renounced their citizenship. With this law on the books, no future Lee Harvey Oswald would be able lawfully to mail order an assassination tool from an out-of-state dealer. The law also said that any imported weapon must have a recognizable "sporting purpose." This helped trigger a long, still continuing, saga of mistrust of federal regulators on the part of those who believe that our weapons rights have both individual and civic purposes, as the Founding Fathers did. Nothing angers a Second Amendment activist more than assuming that "hunting" and "target shooting" are the only acceptable uses for guns, as if guns are merely quaint sporting tools of no more significance than horseshoes or croquet mallets.

The Gun Control Act did leave what has come to be known as the "gun show loophole," which is reviled by anti-gun forces. They find it distasteful that devotees of guns can gather en masse to celebrate fellowship and commerce based on their interest in weapons, military paraphernalia, military history, decorative belt-buckles, and dried meats. The loophole is that various legal restrictions on licensed weapons dealers do *not* apply to any private citizens who might have a gun—or two or three, or maybe four—they want to sell. (No statutory definition states when you are selling enough guns to qualify as a dealer.) Such sales can occur anywhere, not just at gun shows.

Amid the continuing rise in urban crime during the mid-1970s, D.C. passed its Firearms Control Regulations Act in July 1976. The

1970s had seen a further rise in violent crime, from 361.0 to 596.6 incidents per 100,000 population, a 65 percent increase over the course of the decade on top of the 123 percent rise that had already occurred in the 1960s. D.C.'s own homicide rate had tripled in the 1960s. The District already had gun registration as of 1969, and D.C. police were finding 300 unregistered illegal weapons a month in the early 1970s.

The D.C. City Council was feeling its oats in what was only the third year of any sort of home rule. The vote on the FCRA was 12–1. Since D.C. had not yet wrested control of its criminal code from Congress, the FCRA was technically part of D.C.'s health code. This was an interesting presaging of the weird reframing of gun crime since the 1980s—a result of individual choice, however misguided or evil—as a matter of "public health."

Some 50,000 guns had already been registered under the pre-FCRA requirements. They all required re-registration after FCRA, but only 23,000 or so actually were. Two contemporaneous comments from politicians proved prophetic: Republican Rep. Ron Paul of Texas said FCRA was "flat out illegal" and that "this law is going to be challenged, and it is going to be thrown out." Then-councilman, later mayor, Marion Barry, who voted for it anyway, admitted it would "not take one gun out of the hands of one criminal." That statement was not technically true, of course, as D.C. police tend to confiscate 150–200 of them a month (with no appreciable effect on crime or citizens' sense of well-being), but in spirit it was accurate about the degree to which the law would curb D.C.'s violent crime problem.

National attitudes about guns at the time buttressed the D.C. Council's decision, although both Congress and the White House were opposed. D.C.'s Council imagined its regulations would be a bellwether for similarly stringent gun control across the country. It didn't work out that way.

Alan Gottlieb, who had launched his Second Amendment Foundation in Washington State in 1974 (he was already running its sister organization, the Citizens Committee for the Right to Keep and Bear Arms), said that "after the 1968 Gun Control Act, a lot of gun owners were angry and upset. It was a perfect time to organize the gun rights movement. It was the first time in modern history you could do so. We jumped in quickly to do it. The NRA was still more a hunter and safety group, though they launched their ILA [Institute for Legislative Action] [in 1975] in response to the Citizens Committee and Second Amendment Foundation. Of course between '68 and the mid '70s," Gottlieb added, "you saw an awful lot of news stories and editorials in daily papers going after guns and gun rights. That helped us a whole lot. Our opponents helped drive our constituency to us."

The NRA tried its own legal challenge to D.C.'s FCRA regulations; that challenge failed in 1978 in the D.C. Court of Appeals. The NRA was, in that era, riven by infighting over whether the organization should dedicate itself more to politics or to serving the culture of recreational gun use, typified by a plan to move its headquarters to Colorado—a no-no to the political crowd. A plan to change the name of their "national shooting center" to a "national outdoor center" made hardcore gunners think the NRA was getting soft. In November 1976, 74 of the most hardcore gun rights folks at the NRA were summarily fired.

Then in a parliamentary coup at their 1977 annual convention, the more political types retook the NRA, in a maneuver known as the "Cincinnati Revolt" after the city where the convention was held. The NRA from that point on was officially the linchpin of what its opponents sneeringly call the "gun lobby." They were the biggest force in the rise of the New Right, that loose, conflicted, but effective coalition of Reaganism, the religious right, and the anti-tax movement—the whole coalition of bogeymen that made Carter-era liberals blanch. The NRA was in its glory days; from 1977 to 1983 it grew from 1.0 million to 2.6 million members, at times growing by 3,000 members per week.

The NRA has a ferocious reputation for being able to not so much outspend opponents, but to get out its dedicated troops and march them in any direction it commands. It is considered a settled fact in Congress that angering the NRA is a guarantee of a paralyzing flood of angry phone calls and letters.

The NRA's change from sportsmen's support organization to political powerhouse was driven dialectically by its opposite number and arch-foe, the gun-control movement. The NRA didn't have much in the way of organized public opposition to gun-ownership rights to contend with for much of the first century of its history. The organized gun-control movement saw its first long-lasting and successful organization launch in 1974 when Mark Borinsky founded the National Council to Control Handguns, which survives today, after an interregnum as "Handgun Control Inc.," as the Brady Campaign to Prevent Gun Violence. It is an article of faith among NRA types that whatever their surface goals, the true end for professional gun-control activists is eliminating private ownership of handguns entirely (and plenty of comments from gun-control activists help support this fear). Handgun Control Inc. joined, and then later departed from, the National Council to Control Handguns, when it realized that public support was high for gun regulations but not for a total ban.

According to Gregg Lee Carter's book, *The Gun Control Movement*, 20,000 local, county, and state gun control laws passed in the 19th and early 20th centuries. How many different state-level gun laws and regulations are there, and how difficult is it to make meaningful and accurate generalizations about them? Sen. Edward Kennedy (D-MA) used to read aloud hundreds of state gun laws in order to drive away enough of his distinguished colleagues to kill a quorum, according to Osha Grey Davidson in his book about the NRA, *Under Fire*. However, in the past decade or so, the United States has seen a definite trend toward more "shall-issue" concealed carry laws, where citizens who meet certain set criteria can get a license to carry their weapons without any discretion on the part of the issuing authority, with little commensurate carnage.

What localities, states, and the federal government have been doing for decades—with only limited oversight and delimitation by the courts—is this: outlawing the possession and transfer of certain *kinds* of guns; denying certain categories of people the right to own weapons; requiring gun owners to be licensed and to pass exams; and requiring the registration of certain guns. The *Heller* decision is unlikely to change this any time soon.

The civil rights–minded, even those who don't care for guns, should see the potential constitutional problems with such laws. Just think about analogous restrictions on other clearly protected individual rights. For example, should it not be troublesome that someone would need to be licensed, pass a test, or wait to practice their First Amendment right to speak and publish on certain matters—even incendiary matters, such as a manual for hit men or a treatise on bomb making, where some real or imagined civic dangers can be linked to airing certain views or information?

During the 1980s, the gun-rights community saw some legislative victories, but they served as preludes for some crushing defeats in the 1990s. The NRA was pleased with its role in passing the 1986 Firearms Owners Protection Act. That law reduced the penalty for certain record-keeping violations on licensed dealers to a misdemeanor, prohibited national registration of firearms that were not already part of the 1934 NFA, allowed sales of long guns (but still not handguns) to out-of-state residents, and limited inspections of licensed dealers without consent to one a year. On the down side for the NRA crowd, that law also prohibited the manufacture or sale of new machine guns for private use.

Handgun Control Inc. saw the same law as a victory of sorts for gun-control advocates. It did, after all, retain the ban on interstate handgun sales and stopped the sale and manufacture of new machine guns—the first federal ban on any entire class of weapons. (A machine gun is a weapon that can fire more than one bullet per single pull of the trigger. The far more common "semiautomatic" automatically positions a new round with each trigger pull until the clip is empty. Advocates of gun control often elide this distinction, to make people as scared of the somewhat common semiautomatics as they might be of the very rare machine gun.)

The dawning of the Clinton era in the 1990s saw dark days for the NRA and the gun-rights movement. Clinton tended to say the right things to avoid NRA opposition while governor of Arkansas, but when he became president, he turned as anti-gun as any of the NRA's wildest fears. At a California town hall meeting early in his presidency, he advocated "sweeps" as a means to confiscate weapons if necessary. This is the very apotheosis of the fear that lying behind even the most innocuous suggestions for laws to modify, rein in, or regulate the sale and possession of guns lies a secret desire to take them all away.

Gun-control advocates usually like to stick to whatever the particular issue or regulation is at hand and deflect questions about what "next step" they might advocate. Then, when talking to their own constituencies, they will often refer to how any given regulation on the table is not their ultimate goal, but a "good first step." For example, consider what Brady Center founding chair (under its original name, the National Council to Control Handguns) Pete Shields told *The New Yorker* in its July 26, 1976, issue: "The first problem is to slow down the number of handguns being produced and sold. . . . The second problem is to get handguns registered. The final problem is to make possession . . . totally illegal."

Gun registration *has* on occasion been only a "first step" toward confiscation (or attempted confiscation), not only in obvious tyrannies like Nazi Germany, but in liberal democracies including Canada, Great Britain, Australia, and even in California with its state-level "assault weapon" ban in 1989.

In New Orleans after the Hurricane Katrina flooding in 2005, the American people saw vividly—though few seemed to really notice—that at the slightest sign of trouble, even without registration, the government was prepared to blatantly and illegally take people's guns. A sobering video distributed by the NRA of such attempts to disarm people in post-Katrina New Orleans shows police physically tackling and beating an elderly woman just because she held an unloaded revolver in her palm. It also shows them taking and destroying family heirloom weapons in the street from others. These weapons were the only real protection people had in a chaotic situation—the police officers taking the guns were not going to be on the scene later on to help the disarmed citizens in moments of danger.

The Brady Handgun Violence Prevention Act was generally known as the "Brady Bill," named after Ronald Reagan's press secretary James Brady, who was paralyzed after being hit during John Hinckley's shooting of the president in 1981. Its passage in 1993 was a sweet victory for gun-control forces. (In 2001, Handgun Control Inc. renamed itself the Brady Campaign to Prevent Gun Violence.) While it contained some other provisions, such as raising the yearly fee for a federal firearms dealer's license, the Brady Bill's central innovation was the "waiting period." Handgun buyers now had to have their identity reported to local police for a background check and wait five government working days to pick up their gun. The local police were supposed to destroy the information about the buyer after the check, so it wouldn't amount to feared registration. Once the FBI launched its National Instant Criminal Background Check System to determine whether you were eligible to own a gun, the waiting period was phased out (though some states still have them).

Waiting periods were the sort of "minor" regulation meant to seem unobjectionable to all right-minded people. The attitude toward those who opposed this type of restriction was summarized neatly in an episode of *The Simpsons*: Homer becomes a stereotypical gun nut and joins an NRA-style organization. When he goes to buy a weapon and is confronted with the waiting period, he groans, "But I'm angry *now!*"

The Brady Bill's importance was less its effect on the experience of buying or owning a gun in and of itself, but the principle behind it: the law positioned gun purchasing and ownership as not a right, but a privilege, one we can't legally practice without proving ourselves and providing information to the government. This principle so upset the dealer from whom I bought my (legal) handgun in Glendale, California, that he complained about it three times—the injustice of being treated guilty until proven innocent to exercise a simple human right, and a constitutional one.

In September 1994, with the political momentum of the Brady Bill success rolling, Congress passed, and Clinton signed, what was known as the "assault weapons ban," officially the Violent Crime Control and Law Enforcement Act. Gun-rights organizations enjoy pointing at this law when they want to stress the inherently bogus, emotional, and hysteria-based nature of much gun regulation. In the wake of a 1989 Stockton, California, schoolyard massacre and a 1993 San Francisco law office shooting, the legislation targeted a bunch of purely cosmetic features of over 200 models of semiautomatic rifles, shotguns, and pistols.

This measure further confused the general populace on the differences between fully automatic and semiautomatic weaponry, demonized visual features such as folding stocks and bayonet mounts, and targeted weapons that were almost never used in violent crimes, while cementing the principle that there was just "no good reason" why someone would ever need to own certain kinds of guns, with dismissive gags about how "no one needs a weapon like this to shoot deer." From the gun-rights viewpoint, many otherwise law-abiding citizens saw these semiautomatic weapons as a harmless tool of value to their lives and symbolic of their liberty. A total ban was a sign that they were right: The gun-grabbers *were* on the march. Only extreme diligence and activism could stop the next law from hitting, say, *all* semiautomatics, not just the ones with the scary cosmetic elements aimed at by the assault weapons ban.

For all its pointlessness, the law was still a hard sell. The bill passed the Senate by only five votes, and the House by two. Bill

Clinton, savvy politician that he was, later regretted this spate of anti-gun legislation from the Democratic Congress during his first term. He blamed it for the Democrats' bruising loss of control of Congress in 1994.

The assault weapons ban had a sunset provision built in, and with little fanfare it faded out of existence in 2004. Of course, only professional gun dealers or collectors should have even noticed. As Tom Diaz, of the Violence Policy Center, admitted, "If the existing assault weapons ban expires, I personally do not believe it will make one whit of difference" in curbing gun violence. A 1999 National Institute of Justice report on the ban's effect had trouble discerning a result because "the banned weapons and magazines were rarely used to commit murders in this country." The assault weapons ban was born out of cosmetics and ideology, lived that way, then died.

The gun-control debate got muddied in this same era by the association of the gun-rights movement with the "militia movement." This movement made a brief media splash when two people convicted of blowing up the federal building in Oklahoma City in 1995, Timothy McVeigh and Terry Nichols, were said to be fellow travelers of, and influenced by their association with, this loosely affiliated movement of gun-loving eccentric constitutionalists. This group was bound together in part by mistrust of and hatred for the major institution that actually enforces federal gun laws, the Bureau of Alcohol, Tobacco, Firearms and Explosives. As *Parker* plaintiff George Lyon, among the more serious of the gun-culture devotees on the team, quipped, "That should be the name of a convenience store, not a federal enforcement agency."

The BATF were not only doing a job that ought not be done, in the minds of many, but they were also doing it in a clumsy, officious, often even criminal way. Among many less highly publicized instances of overzealous enforcement, heedless of citizens' rights, the BATF was implicated in two huge embarrassments for federal law enforcement. The first was the entrapment and assault of Randy Weaver (and murder of his wife while she held her baby) at Ruby Ridge, Idaho, in 1992. The second, and most extreme such incident, was the botched raid on the Branch Davidian community near Waco, Texas, in 1993 that ended in 82 civilian deaths and 4 BATF agent deaths.

In the 1990s, much of the NRA's and the gun-rights movement's polemical energies were spent grappling with what Wayne LaPierre of the NRA called the "jackbooted thugs" at BATF. The general atmosphere in the gun-rights movement at the time—which was roughly contemporaneous with the Brady Bill and assault weapons ban—was apocalyptic. But it was the darkness before a new dawn in gun rights.

In that era, gun-rights advocacy became blended in the minds of elite opinion with eccentrics playing war games in the woods and possibly plotting terrorist attacks. Mistrust and misunderstanding shadowed the political debate about guns, with both sides glaring dimly at each other across a divide of fact and value.

Gun regulators may believe, for example, that registration is the mildest of possible demands, which only the guilty need fear, as it allows for better and more efficient tracing and tracking of the criminal use of guns. Of course, fewer than 1 percent of extant guns will ever be used in a criminal fashion, as criminologist Gary Kleck explained in his 1991 book *Point Blank: Guns and Violence in America.* In his 2001 book *Armed* (co-authored with Don Kates), Kleck noted that the only supposed benefit of registration that couldn't be obtained through other means is giving governments a list of gun owners. And in the book *Death by Gun Control*, Aaron Zelman thoroughly documented, in populist form (with whiffs of what outsiders might see as hysteria), how registration can be a prelude to confiscation—and confiscation can be a prelude to genocide. Zelman noted that Jews were legally disarmed by Nazi Germany before the program of mass slaughter was launched against them.

No significant new federal legislation regulating weapons sales and possession has made much progress since the Brady Bill and assault weapons ban. Since the 2000 election, when the NRA claimed that they cost Al Gore the presidency, the Democrats have been less enthusiastic about gun restrictions. Representing a widespread view among Democratic politicos and liberal thinkers, *New York Times* columnist Nicholas Kristof wrote in November 2004, "If it weren't for guns, President-elect Kerry might now be conferring with incoming Senate Majority Leader Daschle. Gun control is dead."

This year's Democratic presidential candidate Barack Obama has suffered from his culture-war flub of referring to "bitter" people "clinging" to guns, and he has paid lip service to the individual rights interpretation of the Second Amendment in *Heller*. Obama is still widely reviled in the gun-rights community, with a long history of action, inaction, and chatter that marks him as a potentially dangerous enemy. Obama once answered a questionnaire from an Illinois group saying that he supported total handgun bans. He later backpedaled, claiming an aide had filled it out (though it appeared to be in Obama's handwriting) without consulting him. He has also, as a politician from Chicago, defended that city's own handgun ban against state legislation that would have weakened it and has supported bans on all semiautomatic weapons. Then, in the week after the *Heller* decision came down, Obama tried to position himself where he undoubtedly thinks most Americans are: he declared that, of course, there is an individual right to own a gun, but that that right can be regulated for safety reasons in all sorts of ways.

Nationally, D.C.-style bans are political poison. A Rasmussen poll from June 2008 found that "while there is an even divide on the question of whether stricter laws are needed, only 26 percent believe that city governments have the right to prevent citizens from owning handguns in their city. Sixty-four percent . . . disagree and say such a restriction is a violation of the Second Amendment." Also, "80 percent . . . of Republicans say that city governments should not have the right to ban handguns. That view is shared by 52 percent of Democrats and 63 percent of voters not affiliated with either major party."

However, being against a D.C.-style ban still leaves a lot of room for wondering whether "stricter laws are needed" when it comes to regulating guns. A February 2008 Gallup/*USA Today* poll did find that very close to a majority, 49 percent, of Americans support "more strict" gun laws. Still, that is far fewer than the 78 percent who did so in 1990. (And there is no reason to believe that mass public opinion is well-educated about the realities of what gun laws already exist, how they are enforced, and how they do or don't contribute to public safety.)

I talked to lots of people in the "pro-gun" community, from those who enjoy detonating explosives with semiautomatic rifle fire to dealers in highly regulated states like California. They were abuzz with optimism about the state of the gun-control fight in America this century, and not just because of *Heller*. But the gun-control debate is far from dead, or even dying. Despite *Heller*, gun control could be just one highly publicized public tragedy away from further victories.

While the federal government and its territories were at issue in *Heller*, legislative and court action on gun control has been almost entirely on the state and local level since the gun-control heyday of the mid-1990s. Important trends have both expanded and contracted weapons rights in the United States since then.

America has seen a huge increase in the number of states shifting to what's called a "shall issue" system for permits to carry concealed weapons. "Shall issue," now the standard in 37 states (up from only 8 in 1986), means that if the applicant meets a set standard requirement—generally just being a law-abiding adult who has taken a certified safety course and has no history of institutionaliza-tion—then the government officials have to issue the license. (Of course, with the usual hypocrisy by which the state takes care of its own, police officers and retired police officers can carry guns concealed anywhere, under federal law. And D.C.'s gun ban exempts members of Congress.)

"Shall issue" is the opposite of the discretionary permit system, exemplified by New York's Sullivan Law, whereby authorities can decide whether they think you need or deserve to be able to carry a weapon. In some localities with such requirements, this means that only people with the right connections can carry a gun. The publisher of the very anti-gun *New York Times*, Arthur Sulzberger Jr., has a carry permit in New York. When I bought my own first gun in the L.A. metro area, I went through the two hours of tests and paperwork before paying for the weapon—which I was not able to take home with me for 10 days under California state law. When I innocently asked about the possibility of getting a carry permit, the dealer just guffawed. Of course, prominent celebrity gun foes such as Rosie O'Donnell pay professionals—with guns—to guard them. This sort of blatant hypocrisy on the part of gun-control advocates shows that nearly everyone, short of the very few sincere pacifists, understands that guns *are* a vital self-defense tool—just one that some people think others shouldn't be able to have, as if their lives are worth less.

The gun-control movement's efforts since the 1990s have been aimed not so much at passing new laws, but toward lawsuits against gun manufacturers and sellers for harms caused by the people who misuse the weapons. This strategy, which was almost never success-ful, caused a backlash in state houses, where 33 states barred such suits by legislative action. This wave of lawsuits was brought to an end when Congress passed the 2005 Protection of Lawful Commerce in Arms Act (which also, as a legislative compromise, contained a handgun safety lock requirement).

Although they may deny the connection between markets and liberty in the broadest terms, gun opponents do understand that freedoms are meaningless without the physical ability to practice them. Freedom to keep and bear arms belongs to those able to obtain them, and anything that makes guns more expensive or difficult or just aggravating to get limits that freedom. Thus, groups like the Brady Center have lately aimed legal action at gun dealers for supposed negligence in allowing weapons to fall into criminal hands—and at forcing manufacturers to lard their product with more safety features, thereby making guns more expensive than they otherwise would be.

In New Jersey, as one would-be gun owner complained on the legal blog "Concurring Opinions" in June 2008, "I first need to obtain a 'Firearms Purchaser Identification Card.' This involves release of any mental health records, giving the names and addresses of two non-family references who apparently have to vouch for you (whose business is it if I want to buy a gun?), and be fingerprinted and have a full FBI background check completed. Then I have to apply for a separate Pistol Permit. Approval of this is apparently at the whim of your local chief of police who can deny it for any reason and not tell you why. The whole process can take months even though it's supposed to be within 30 days by law and costs close to $100 total."

That's nearly 20 hours of work, half a week's wage after tax for minimum wage laborers. This sort of barrier, far short of a D.C.-level ban, is why people like Kenn Blanchard, the "Black Man With a Gun," see potential racism and classism in stringent gun controls that make it more difficult, time-consuming, and expensive to get a weapon for personal defense.

Things had gotten better nationally for gun owners in the past decade, but in certain localities and states (gun-rights advocates point to Illinois, Massachusetts, New Jersey, and California as among the worst) severe restrictions on sales, ownership, and carry of weapons persisted. According to FBI statistics, the annual number of arrests for pure weapons law violations increased 21 percent from

2000 to 2005. And no municipality had held so close, for so long, to the vision of a city completely without usable legal guns as the District of Columbia.

On February 10, 2003, the six plaintiffs gathered by Bob Levy and his team officially filed their challenge to several of D.C.'s firearm statutes in U.S. District Court for the District of Columbia, charging that those laws violated their Second Amendment rights. With Shelly Parker as the lead plaintiff, *Parker v. District of Columbia* was now officially alive.

D.C. city officials were fond of their gun control, were loath to give up on it, and had even apparently managed to convince themselves that it had done some good for the city. They did not take kindly to a challenge from this gang of freelance upstarts. Then-Mayor Anthony Williams's office told the *Washington Times* the week the suit was announced, "You're not going to see any will on the part of this mayor to relax the gun laws in the District." Yet D.C.'s legal team didn't seem to be taking the case as seriously as it merited.

Someone in the D.C. attorney general's office had quit; someone else failed to make sure the case ended up on top of anyone else's pile. The case had literally been forgotten. For a while, as Levy's team recalled, no one in the D.C. government was working on it at all. Such legal neglect isn't exactly unusual for the District, Clark Neily said. "We filed a motion for summary judgment within a couple of months after the case was filed. No doubt D.C. knew about the case; it was on the front pages of the *Washington Post* and *Washington Times.* A very important, high profile case and . . . it slipped through the cracks, was assigned to a lawyer who left the office and went unmanaged." D.C. missed the deadline to respond to the summary judgment request—but got an extension until June.

Neily marveled:

> If you were a lawyer in private practice, the first call after you did that would be to your malpractice team to alert them a claim was coming. Judges generally are not forgiving. To go to court and say we failed to file a response to this important motion because we weren't managing our lawyers well, we dropped the ball—D.C. gets that slack all the time. It's astonishing. There's this unwritten rule that two separate standards apply: to lawyers for D.C. and all other lawyers. Lawyers for D.C. are used to always getting a break. Missed deadline? No problem! Didn't get ducks in a row? Go ahead,

have a second try. If a regular law firm came to court and said 'We failed to file a critical brief in a high profile case because an associate left for another firm and we didn't pick up his case load, we just left it on his desk'—we'd get laughed out of court.

Could it be, I asked Neily, that D.C. wasn't really taking the case seriously? He smiled. "The experience I've had, the difference between the D.C. attorney general's office taking it really seriously and just litigating like any old case is not that great."

D.C.'s government was not alone in thinking the suit should never have been filed. The *Heller* case faced another enemy, one in some ways even more formidable than D.C. Strangely, this enemy was what most people think of as the most tenacious and longest-lasting defender of Americans' gun rights: the National Rifle Association. This surprised nearly every layperson I discussed this case with, most of whom assumed the NRA was behind filing the lawsuit in the first place. The NRA's duel with the case got very little press as it unfolded; one interesting exception is "Gun Fight," an article in *Washington Lawyer*'s July/August 2007 issue by Joan Indiana Rigdon.

Early in the planning process, in August 2002, members of Levy's team got a visit from George Mason University Law Professor Nelson Lund and prominent Washington lawyer Chuck Cooper, both associated with the NRA. Both had long histories of defending gun liberties, in academic and popular writings and in court. Both were firm believers in the individual rights interpretation of the Second Amendment. But they thought what Levy and his team were trying was, right then and there, too risky and could end up harming the cause of Second Amendment rights more than helping it.

Lund and Cooper did not explicitly say that they were representing the NRA and wanted this lawsuit to die in the cradle. But they did try to sell their comrades on the idea that this was the wrong lawsuit at the wrong time, that the Court (which, at the time, had Justice Sandra Day O'Connor sitting in the place Justice Samuel Alito now occupies) did not have a reliable five votes for their side, and that a definitive loss on the Second Amendment's meaning could seriously damage the gun-rights fight in the courts at every other level.

Levy and his crew could understand this argument, but they were not swayed. *Any* reasonable consideration of the idea that we have an individual right to hold guns would lead ineluctably, under any standard of review, to the conclusion that D.C.'s gun ban was an egregious violation of that right.

Alan Gura had a bit of sympathy for the NRA's position—just a bit. The NRA had adopted a "more cautious" approach to pushing Second Amendment arguments, mostly trying to avoid high-level judicial confrontations that might, after all, end up with a wrong-headed precedent on the books. "That was a good strategy in its day," Gura told me. "But its day ended with *Emerson. Emerson* finally made it likely that the Supreme Court would have to reach the [Second Amendment] issue. We didn't think [the Second Amendment fight] was optional any more."

As nearly everyone who pays attention to the NRA told me, but no one who works for them closely will say on the record, a more complicated reason might have buttressed the NRA's desire to see Levy's lawsuit sidelined. Gura noted, "The second problem the NRA had with our case was territorial. They didn't want something like this going on that they didn't have their hands in. I think our reputations and backgrounds speak for themselves. At the very least, none of us are crazy or sloppy people. But, nonetheless, the NRA's confidence level [about the case] would have been higher if it were someone in-house [arguing it] so they filed a copycat case."

The NRA and the libertarians had a complicated relationship. The NRA paints itself as America's longest-lived civil rights organization, but its vision of civil rights is narrower than the libertarian's. Libertarians like Levy and his crew stand for the full panoply of rights both explicit and inherent in the Constitution. The NRA at times lets its vision of rights be more narrowly focused on the rights and interests of weapons owners—and sometimes manufacturers and sellers.

Thus, as Levy explained it, he and his colleagues, while finding common cause with the NRA on Second Amendment matters, found themselves opposed to the NRA on such issues as the 2005 NRA-pushed Protection of Lawful Commerce in Arms Act, which restricted government and private tort lawsuits against gun dealers or manufacturers for the harmful use of their products by others. Levy opposed this measure because it ran afoul of the constitutional principle of federalism, arguing that state tort law is not properly the federal government's concern. He also disagreed with the NRA's advocacy for the principle that private employers shouldn't be able to bar their employees from having guns in their parking lots. For many libertarians and conservatives, that's a property rights issue. The employer's right to set rules on his property outweighs the gun-owner's ability to have his gun with him wherever he wishes. (On the other side of the debate, the generally liberal gun-control advocate suddenly finds himself an avid defender of a businessman's property rights, not a position those types generally take.)

Neily also thought it was urgent to take on the inevitable Second Amendment Supreme Court fight on *their* terms, something he believed the NRA didn't properly understand. "My sense," he said, "is the NRA's preference was to let the issue continue to percolate in appeals courts, get some more circuits to come around. And that's an absolutely valid approach. That's how civil rights cases went forward, ending up with *Brown v. Board of Education*.

"But it's dangerous to impose one model on all situations," Neily said. "I saw a couple of problems with that approach for the Second Amendment." At the time, only the Fifth Circuit had accepted the individual rights view of the Second Amendment. So for an incremental approach to work, Neily noted, "you'd have to get circuits to override existing cases. It was also a race against time in the sense that criminal defendants were trying to get a case to the Supreme Court while you are doing your incremental strategy."

It wasn't that the NRA didn't believe in using the courts to vindicate gun owners' rights when they thought a law overstepped constitutional bounds. They just didn't use the Second Amendment as a tool to do so. Before *Heller*, the Second Amendment had been so moribund in the courts they thought it an ineffective argument. Stephen Halbrook himself had won significant victories involving weapons-related laws or prosecutions, some even at the Supreme Court. He defeated a Columbus, Ohio, assault weapon ban in a federal appeals court in a 1996 case *People's Rights Organization v. Columbus* on grounds of vagueness. At the Supreme Court he won, among other cases, *Printz v. United States* (1997), a challenge to the Brady Bill mandate that local officials conduct background checks. That case was won on Tenth Amendment grounds, as an illegitimate command to local officials.

But the Second Amendment could no longer be evaded by friend or foe. The Supreme Court had to stop hiding from it after *Emerson,* or at least it was very likely that the Court would grant review if gun-rights advocates could secure a victory in another federal circuit court. And if the Supreme Court were to revisit the Second Amendment, it would be better for the plaintiff to be a law-abiding security guard who wanted to defend himself in his home. The far worse alternative was someone who had used an unregistered illegal handgun in a carjacking and wanted to knock a couple of years off his sentence by asking a court to invalidate the gun-violation charge on the basis of the Second Amendment.

The NRA's stated motivations for objecting to *Parker* were intellectually respectable, the Levy team thought, but ultimately too fearful and rearguard. If no one was willing to fight for the Second Amendment qua Second Amendment in a case where it would count, then its supposed champions were as complicit in its continued deep sleep as the most rabid partisan for the idea that "the Second Amendment only applied to militias and is thus a dead letter."

What, Levy wondered, did they really have to lose? Levy approached the case with a bit of a riverboat gambler's mentality, to be sure—no one would say that mounting a Second Amendment challenge after 64 years of *Miller* was a gimme. But he had some skill at counting the cards. Levy saw *Emerson*; he saw a Justice Department that was, at least in theory, on his side; he saw the manifest empirical failure of D.C.'s ban, a ban that in severity went far beyond almost any other state or locality; and he saw that even prominent liberal legal scholars had made bold turnarounds on the Second Amendment's meaning. And he had a healthy, sensible, almost mordant sense as to what he and his side had to lose versus the potential damage to D.C. or to the general principle that gun regulations presented no constitutional issues that any legislator had to take seriously.

After all, it was already settled precedent in all but one of the federal judicial circuits that no individual right to gun ownership existed in the Second Amendment—the Fifth Circuit after *Emerson* was the only exception. And lots of the best decisions in the courts protecting gun rights in the past few decades had been based not on the federal Constitution, but on state constitutions: 43 of them included provisions protecting gun rights, many of which were either explicitly stronger than the federal one or were taken more seriously by state courts.

As Gene Healy noted, "Sure, it would be bad to have a definitive statement from the Supreme Court that the Second Amendment doesn't protect an individual right. But except in the Fifth Circuit it's hard to see what the practical impact would be. It leaves you more or less where you were before."

The Levy team was up against a foe with essentially bottomless pockets, without the help—and indeed, they suspected, with the active interference—of the most powerful and successful organization standing for the rights they thought they were fighting to vindicate. But Gura was ready for the fight and set about making himself an expert on gun law and the Second Amendment. In addition to the caselaw he had to master, he "read an awful lot of law review articles, all the standard ones that people talk about. Don Kates has a seminal law review article in the *Michigan Law Review* published in 1983 ('Handgun Prohibition and the Original Meaning of the Second Amendment') about handgun prohibition, and that was a fantastic resource. From there, if it's been written about the Second Amendment, I probably read it. We certainly didn't start from scratch. These issues were written about heavily, researched by other people in the field. It was useful to have the several lifetimes of research other people had gone through so I did not have to go into musty old libraries full of 19th-century texts, if someone else had already done that. Even that's easy to do these days, with everything digitized. You can recall on your desktop some wonderful musty old treatise."

By April 4, 2003, less than two months after *Parker*'s filing, it was no longer the *only* legal challenge to D.C. gun laws being pursued in D.C.'s District Court. With the backing of the NRA and with its longtime legal eagle and Second Amendment scholar Stephen Halbrook in charge, a new lawsuit, *Seegars v. Ashcroft*, was filed.

As per then-standard NRA practice, given their doubts about the efficacy of Second Amendment arguments, Halbrook offered the court a menu of options to choose from to overthrow D.C. gun laws, hoping one of them might work even if a direct Second Amendment challenge might not. One claim stated that Congress had only empowered D.C., as a federal enclave, to create for itself regulations that were "usual and reasonable," and D.C.'s gun laws were, as the most severe ones in the nation, unusual and unreasonable.

Another stated that the registration requirement violated due process by authorizing an act only under a certain condition—registration—and refusing to let that condition be fulfilled. Halbrook also claimed that D.C.'s laws failed to provide equal protection under the law, since nonresidents were allowed to bring in legally registered handguns for recreational use while residents were not.

The NRA also searched for clients among its known community of citizens interested in gun rights. It found five who all lived in crime-ridden neighborhoods and had experiences with burglaries or muggings. The lead plaintiff, Sandra Seegars, was, like Shelly Parker, a black woman living in a neighborhood where violent crime with guns was common.

Seegars worked for the city's own Taxicab Commission. She once made a public splash by suggesting that the city allow taxi drivers to arm themselves for protection from criminals. That proposal inspired then-Mayor Williams's spokesman to tell the *Washington Post* that "the proposal is nutty, and obviously, it would not be entertained seriously by any thinking person." This example pretty vividly illustrates the often unbridgeable gap between pro- and anti-gun-rights forces.

Unlike the Levy team, Halbrook and the NRA chose to sue not only D.C. but the federal Department of Justice perhaps hoping that the DOJ's stated belief in an individual right in the Second Amendment might sway its reaction. However, the DOJ turned out to be a more formidable opponent than D.C.

Next, adding insult to injury because of its unease with Levy and his inexperienced crew, the NRA team used *Seegars* as an excuse to try to scuttle *Parker* by taking over the case, through the legal gambit of "consolidation." That's when two cases that are asking courts to decide on essentially the same matter can be combined, whether or not one of the parties really wants it—a hostile takeover of the litigation, as it were. Levy strongly opposed this hostile takeover because, if the NRA took over the case, it would likely strangle the proverbial baby in the crib. The NRA did not believe the time was right for a Second Amendment case to go to the Supreme Court. Since it could not persuade Levy to give up his planned lawsuit, it was now trying to scuttle Levy's suit. Fortunately, Halbrook's consolidation request, made to the court in April 2003, failed.

Cases crawl through court dockets at an unpredictable pace, one that litigants can't fully control. Moreover, D.C. got a 60-day extension to respond to the Levy team's motion for summary judgment because they had had no lawyer working the case for some time. As a result, *Seegars* ended up dismissed by the District Court and in the appeals process with the U.S. Court of Appeals for the D.C. Circuit before *Parker* was through the District Court.

At the District Court, in January 2004, all but one *Seegars* plaintiff—one with a registered shotgun contesting the trigger-lock aspect of D.C.'s laws—were denied standing; and another one had her Second Amendment claim tossed by Judge Reggie Walton on a basic "she isn't in a militia" argument. Halbrook and the NRA appealed.

D.C. had filed a motion to dismiss Levy's *Parker* lawsuit in March 2003, and on March 31, 2004, D.C. won: The *Parker* suit was dismissed by U.S. District Judge Emmet Sullivan on a straight "*Miller* says Second Amendment rights only apply to militias, these six aren't in a militia, so they have no case" argument. Levy appealed. But then, because the D.C. Circuit Court of Appeals decided that the issues in both cases were essentially the same—that is, a ruling in *Seegars* would also make clear what the ruling in *Parker* would be—the court halted the appeals progress of *Parker*, at D.C.'s request, pending resolution of *Seegars*. In effect, the NRA had taken over the litigation, as it planned.

At the D.C. Circuit Court in a February 2005 decision, *Seegars* ran aground, wrecked on the rock of standing—a person's legal qualification to sue to challenge a law. Thus, the damaging question of client standing was dragged into the D.C. gun lawsuits—another grievance Gura had against the NRA for sticking its nose in his case, and the thing he grew to regret the most about the aborted *Seegars*.

The Levy team had chosen very deliberately to challenge only misdemeanors associated with D.C.'s gun laws, since misdemeanors are enforced by District officials. They kept the federal DOJ out of it and were glad to do so.

"Why," Gura wondered, "sue a defendant that is very sharp and very skilled when you can sue—and there's no nice way to say this . . . the city has lots of turnover in lawyers, and we saw that here. We don't think they bring the same resources to a case the federal DOJ brings, and you just don't pick fights with unnecessary defendants."

Gura thought the NRA team believed that suing Ashcroft

> would somehow cause him to oppose the law, or say 'Oh
> yes, it's unconstitutional.' But as it turned out suing the DOJ
> was almost fatal to our case, because it was the DOJ that
> came up with the standing thing, while the D.C. government
> had not thought of it. In fact, they didn't think about it
> even *after* the *Seegars* case got knocked out. This is how
> lackadaisical D.C.'s preparation for the case was. When we
> went to court at our hearing on our motion for summary
> judgment to dismiss, we knew the judge would talk about
> standing because it was key to the other case [*Seegars*]. But
> the city was not prepared to discuss it. So the standing issue
> was fully a DOJ invention, a creative invention, and one that
> almost proved fatal to us—and *was* fatal to the NRA. And
> had they not sued Ashcroft their case would have gotten
> farther, so that was a critical strategic error on their part.

Despite living in dangerous neighborhoods with specific histories of having their well-being or property threatened, the court decided that none of the *Seegars* plaintiffs had a legitimate cause of action against D.C. But because the decision was based on the technicality of standing as opposed to the legal merits of the arguments, it did not directly harm *Parker*'s ability to move forward in the D.C. Circuit Court. Once again, *Parker* stood alone. The NRA's obstructions, however, were not over. The strategic aftermath of the decision to bring in Ashcroft harmed *Parker* as well. The D.C. Circuit Court of Appeals, in coming down with its *Parker* decision on March 9, 2007, booted five of the original plaintiffs off the case, for the same reason that the five *Seegars* plaintiffs were all tossed away. Sure, Parker and her compatriots might *think* that a core, fundamental, constitutional right was being denied them because of the laws, policies, and arrest threats of the defendant District of Columbia. But, by the D.C. Circuit Court's standard, they had suffered no specific injury such that they had the right to sue. In the legal lingo, they lacked "standing."

The D.C. Circuit Court has a peculiar and absurdly stringent position on the legal doctrine of standing. A 1997 case, ironically involving a gun manufacturer, *Navegar v. United States*, established the principle that plaintiffs must, in the language of D.C.'s filing to dismiss the plaintiffs in *Parker*, "demonstrate a threat of prosecution that is 'credible and immediate,' or imminent, and 'not merely abstract or speculative.'" The chilling effect of knowing a law exists

MARCH 18, 2008. People began lining up long before dawn at the U.S. Supreme Court building to try to obtain one of the few seats available to the public to witness the oral arguments that would begin at 10 a.m. in *District of Columbia v. Heller*.

A resident of Georgetown, one of Washington's most affluent communities, GILLIAN ST. LAWRENCE is interviewed by a reporter at the Supreme Court. St. Lawrence became a plaintiff after meeting attorney Clark Neily at a legal conference. "Yes, you have to deal with the unpleasant fact that someone might break into your house and want to kill you with a gun," she says.

In February 2002, plaintiff SHELLY PARKER moved to a neighborhood near Capitol Hill that was being menaced by drug gangs. In response to her efforts to make the neighborhood safer, her car window was smashed, a security camera she had installed was stolen, a gang member rammed a car into her back fence, and one drug dealer threatened, "Bitch, I'll kill you. I live on this block, too." Despite the violence around her home, lawyers for the city made it clear that they were prepared to arrest and prosecute Parker if she were to keep a gun for her own protection.

GEORGE LYON, a communications lawyer and plaintiff, is keenly aware of the grave responsibility that comes with choosing to use a gun against a criminal. "The last thing you want to do is use your weapon for self-defense," he says. "But if you don't have it, then you could die, or someone you love could die."

TRACY HANSON, a federal employee with the Department of Agriculture and a plaintiff in the case, first heard about the lawsuit through her husband, Andrew. Andrew Hanson learned the details of the planned lawsuit during a chance encounter with an NRA official in a sporting goods store parking lot in a Virginia suburb of Washington, D.C.

TOM PALMER, a plaintiff in the case, is interviewed by local media following the federal appeals court ruling against the District's gun ban in March 2007. More than a decade earlier, he and a friend were cornered by a gang of men who threatened: "We're going to kill you. They'll never find your bodies." Fortunately, Palmer was carrying a handgun for protection. He brandished it and told the trouble-makers to "back up to the other side of the street and go the other way." They complied.

ROBERT LEVY is an attorney and senior fellow in constitutional studies at the Cato Institute. Levy recruited the team of lawyers, led the search for plaintiffs, financed the case, and turned the idea of challenging the District of Columbia's gun ban into a landmark constitutional precedent.

Plaintiffs' attorney **ALAN GURA**, speaking at a Cato Institute event on March 22, 2007. Cato hosted a special public forum entitled "D.C. Gun Ban in the Cross Hairs."

The plaintiffs' legal team at a press conference at the Supreme Court on the morning of June 26, 2008, following the announcement of the Court's historic decision, its first ruling on the Second Amendment in 70 years. Pictured: **CLARK NEILY**, at center, is flanked by **ROBERT LEVY** (at left) and **ALAN GURA** (at right).

D.C. Police Chief **CATHY L. LANIER** (left) and D.C. Mayor **ADRIAN M. FENTY** (right), standing before members of the city council, speak at a press conference on the steps of city hall on June 26, 2008, reacting to the news of their legal defeat at the Supreme Court. When a federal appeals court ruled in March 2007, that the Second Amendment protects an individual's right to keep and bear arms, Mayor Fenty told reporters he was "outraged" by the decision.

JUNE 26, 2008. The *Heller* case touched the emotions, beliefs, and energies of individuals and groups on all sides of the gun rights issue. Above, gun rights opponents display signs at the Supreme Court as the press is briefed on the Court's ruling, while, pictured below, advocates for gun rights mounted their own demonstration.

THE SUPREME COURT. First row, left to right: Justice **ANTHONY M. KENNEDY**, Justice **JOHN PAUL STEVENS**, Chief Justice **JOHN G. ROBERTS**, Justice **ANTONIN SCALIA**, Justice **DAVID H. SOUTER**. Second row, left to right: Justice **STEPHEN G. BREYER**, Justice **CLARENCE THOMAS**, Justice **RUTH BADER GINSBURG** and Justice **SAMUEL ALITO**.

By a razor thin 5-4 vote, the Supreme Court ruled that the District of Columbia's gun control laws violated the Second Amendment of the Constitution. The majority opinion was authored by Justice Antonin Scalia and was joined by Justices Roberts, Kennedy, Thomas, and Alito. Justices Stevens, Souter, Ginsburg, and Breyer dissented.

AUGUST 18, 2008. Like his fellow plaintiffs, **DICK HELLER** wanted to be able to keep a handgun in his home for the purpose of self-defense. After five long years of battling city hall in courtrooms, supported by a committed legal team, he succeeded. The Supreme Court ruling forced city officials to change their laws to allow residents to keep firearms in their homes. Here, less than eight weeks after the Supreme Court's decision, Heller gestures victory as he displays his newly approved gun permit.

barring your desired activity isn't enough, D.C. wrote. More or less, D.C. said that since the plaintiffs might be able to *get away* with breaking the gun laws, since they didn't *know for sure* they'd end up in the pokey, they had no standing to challenge those laws.

Levy's team pointed out that surely no court would allow a law against reading books in the home to be held to this sort of standing standard. Still, the D.C. Circuit Court chose to interpret the *Navegar* standing principle stringently. Only one of the original six plaintiffs survived the standing challenge and became, not by anyone's choice, the one and only official plaintiff and poster boy for the case: Dick Heller.

How is it that Heller, among all his fellow plaintiffs and the *Seegars* crew, survived the standing challenge? Even before the case was officially filed, his friend Dane vonBreichenruchardt knew Heller was involved and intending to be a plaintiff—he had offered him up to Levy himself. VonBreichenruchardt was familiar with how troublesome the standing question could be. He had been a plaintiff in a previous case against certain regulations affecting the operations of nonprofits, ones that he thought amounted to a prior restraint on his First Amendment rights. He wanted to defy the law—to send a solicitation letter before the laws constraining his nonprofit allowed him to—but was advised by his partners in the case not to bother. Partly because of this, he saw the case dismissed for lack of standing. So vonBreichenruchardt encouraged Heller to do something that was, on the surface, pointless: he told him to go down to the gun control office at the police station on Indiana Ave., NW, and fill out the form to try to register one of the handguns Heller owned but stored away from his District home.

That act turned out to be one of the most *important* futile, pointless, meaningless bureaucratic gestures in American history. Without that sad, ignored, rejected piece of government-issued paper, a copy of which was dutifully attached to all the early filings in the case of *Parker v. District of Columbia,* not a single one of the carefully selected squad of six would have been legally considered to have had standing. That is, they had not suffered an injury such that they could sue D.C. for prohibiting them from exercising their Second Amendment rights—if indeed they *had* any Second Amendment rights, a question which the courts had yet to settle.

Neily, who like all the lawyers on the case considers the *Navegar* standing doctrine outrageous and sure to eventually fall to a court challenge, is still amazed. "It makes all the difference in the world this one guy went down and filled out an absolutely meaningless piece of paper which you knew in advance was a futile act! It was not intentional on the part of Alan, Bob, and myself, but it was intentional on the part of Dick and Dane, and it was very important that Dane had that insight and did that."

By any standard, the notion that his clients had no reasonable fear of prosecution was absurd, Gura thought. "I told the judge, in open court, we can resolve this easily: Ask the city if they intend to prosecute our clients! The judge said, sure, I know the answer, but I'll ask anyway. So he asked the city's lawyer. 'Would you prosecute if they violated the law?' 'Of course we will. If they violate the law, we will in fact prosecute.'

"I said, 'There's your threat by the city's lawyer to enforce the law against these specific people,' and the D.C. Circuit [Court] still wouldn't accept that. The city had all sorts of explanations [for the lawyer's public threat], saying he was a civil counsel and he doesn't actually prosecute, he really doesn't know what our prosecutors would do."

Dick Heller slid in because he had a permit denied: a clear injury with a paper trail. That was great, in that it kept the case alive, but it was still completely ridiculous, Gura insisted. "Because it's a registration system and you're not allowed to register a handgun, the case goes forward. But the city could just as easily draw up a law saying, forget registration, all guns are illegal. Make firearms like drugs: it's just illegal to have them. You can't register them." Then, somehow, *no one* could have standing to challenge the laws? That's patently absurd. Gura continued, "There are many laws challenged in America the day they are enacted or the day they go into effect. The Communications Decency Act, restrictions on partial birth abortion—no one is waiting for a prosecution [on those]. The government could have taken the position, 'We've never prosecuted a partial birth abortion case. Maybe we'll ignore [the law]. How do you know we're going to go after you? You don't even have a client who needs a partial birth abortion. You're just a doctor. Are you pregnant?' No one stopped for one minute to think of that. Of course they have standing."

That they faced no real threat of prosecution was news to Gillian St. Lawrence. As the case crawled through the courts, she attended a public meeting at a school auditorium in July 2005 focused on gun regulations with some D.C. officials speaking, including then-Mayor Williams and then-Chief of Police Charles Ramsey. "We are sitting there, and we hear these threats about no tolerance, no exception for self-defense, you use anything and you are gonna go to jail. And for them to tell us they won't enforce it? I walked out of that meeting scared to death that I'll go to jail if I use [my shotgun at home]."

VonBreichenruchardt is conscious—*acutely* conscious—of how important this act of Heller's, this act which they both agree Heller wouldn't have gone through without the worried Dane's prodding, was to the case's fate and eventual victory. He feels like he has a huge stake in his friend's legal battle, indeed even a claim of ownership, a stake that hasn't been properly reflected in the public talk and media coverage of the case. As Heller puts it, he considers himself to have been originally a client of the Bill of Rights Foundation in its early plans to challenge D.C.'s gun laws, just one who was handed over to the Levy crew.

VonBreichenruchardt wants the Bill of Rights Foundation to be more prominently mentioned in discussing the case's genesis and process. He suspects (and he's pretty much right) that the legal team in *Heller* would rather avoid media focus on him and his wide-ranging constitutional concerns, not wanting to muddy the waters of this clean, precise, narrow case they crafted.

Heller and vonBreichenruchardt remember something about that day—July 17, 2002—that the case was saved by Dick Heller's filling out a form. As he was walking away, they recall, the officer on duty in the gun-control office said to him, "Good luck with your case, Mr. Heller." He knew exactly what they were up to, vonBreichenruchardt and Heller insist.

A similar understanding (or suspicion) was most likely on the minds of the clerks at D.C.'s gun registration office when they refused even to give the necessary paperwork to Tom Palmer when he tried to register a gun in June 2007. He found out he had to bring the unregistered firearm to the police station where the registration office was. Who is going to do such an insane thing? he wondered. He was told that if he was stopped, he should just tell the officer he was bringing the gun in to be registered. But when he said he wanted to register a pistol, not a legal long gun, the clerk literally snatched the form from his hand. Would she be willing to write

67

down that she was refusing to let him even fill out the form? Palmer asked. The woman on duty refused. He was given no explanation. One woman he was talking to, he recalls, flipped her badge around so he couldn't even get her name.

How was such a smart team of lawyers outsmarted on this standing issue? "It's easy to say, 'Why was the NRA so dumb, why were we so dumb?'" Gura said. "But you can't do it. It's a Catch-22. You can't apply for registration of an imaginary gun. You have to *have* a gun, and you can't buy a gun in D.C. And there's a *federal* law that says you can't buy a handgun anywhere except the state you live in. If you live in D.C., you can't go to Maryland and buy a handgun. No one will sell you one. You can't go to Virginia and buy one either. So if you live in D.C. and want standing, either you break the law and get prosecuted, then vindicate your rights, which is an absurd standing argument, or temporarily move from D.C., change your state of residence, and buy a handgun, then move *back* into D.C. You can't bring your handgun with you, but you can bring paperwork proving you own it, and that's what Heller did." Heller was able to prove that he owned a handgun that he had purchased when he lived outside D.C.

Neily, with his years of experience in public interest litigation defending constitutional rights, said he was "flummoxed" by the D.C. Circuit Court's booting of the five plaintiffs. "What would you have to do to get standing? Buy an illegal handgun, drive up and down in front of the D.C. police department waving it out the window and screaming that you don't have registration for this? Then when a prosecutor comes out with an indictment in his hands, you have to beat him to federal court! Because once a proceeding is initiated against you in a local court system, your right to be in federal court is gone. You'd literally have to provoke a threat and somehow beat them to the federal courthouse." That's because of an obscure doctrine whereby federal courts will not entertain a civil challenge while a local criminal case is in progress. "The D.C. court was basically saying there is no real set of circumstances under which" anyone who didn't already own a handgun could challenge D.C.'s gun laws in federal court.

Standing wasn't the only matter the D.C. Circuit Court decided on March 9, 2007. Their other action that day was better news for the *Parker* team. In what Levy acknowledged was a lucky break for the case, they ended up at the Circuit Court of Appeals with a three-judge panel consisting of Laurence Silberman, Karen Henderson, and Thomas Griffith. "We happened to get three conservative-leaning judges," Levy said. "You can't always predict by political inclination, but I think we got an edge with Silberman and Griffith. I thought we had Henderson, too, but that turned out to not be the edge I thought we had, because Henderson dissented. But it was still much better than getting three liberal judges."

The oral arguments had been heard on December 7, 2006. In that March 9, 2007, decision Dick Heller's rights (and by extension those of Shelly Parker and his other fellow original plaintiffs) were vindicated. The Second Amendment still lived.

Judge Laurence H. Silberman wrote the opinion for the three-judge panel. In a 2-1 vote, they ordered the case back to the District Court with a directive: grant summary judgment to Heller, meaning, he wins.

The decision caught D.C.'s Mayor Adrian Fenty totally by surprise. He was, he told the *Washington Post*, "frankly outraged" that a court dared to presume that the citizens of his city might be able to take self-defense into their own hands. The *Post* joined him in his anger, declaring it in an editorial "unconscionable . . . to give individuals Second Amendment rights."

The Silberman opinion was a glorious, sweet victory for the Levy team and for the Second Amendment. Silberman hit all the right points. He struck at the authority of all the federal appellate courts who have said the Second Amendment protects no individual right by pointing out that at least seven state appeals courts—whose interpretations, he insisted, are no less authoritative than those of other federal appeals courts—have agreed an individual right is contained in the amendment. He decided that the "people" in the amendment meant *the people*, that is, all of us as individuals. He decided that "bear arms" had more than just a military meaning in the idiom of the founding era. He noted the "sophisticated collective rights theory" posited by D.C., but blew it away by noting that it was the functional equivalent of the old collective rights theory—that the Second Amendment right applies to states, not individuals—in that it claims that the individual only has a Second Amendment right in connection with his *membership* in a state militia. He also noted that the militia, in the Founding context, consisted of pretty much all able-bodied men, not a select group.

Silberman stood up for his court's right and ability to rethink the Second Amendment afresh, saying he felt no square precedent had been set in their circuit, nor by the Supreme Court. His decision interpreted *Miller*, the apparent dominant precedent, to say it hinged on the type of weapon the right affected, not the type of person. Silberman did not accept D.C.'s claim that any constitutional infringement was mitigated because the city *might not* punish a long gun owner for loading and using his weapon in self-defense in defiance of the letter of the law—"judicial leniency cannot make up for the unreasonable restriction of a right."

The decision was well-reasoned, but it was only from one three-judge panel of the D.C. Circuit. D.C. officials requested a rehearing by the entire body of judges for the Circuit, known as a rehearing *en banc*. That request was denied in May 2007. The city then requested, and got, a stay on the order to stop enforcing its law while it decided whether it wished to take the case on to the next step: the Supreme Court of the United States.

The decision in *Heller* was ultimately—and appropriately—based on legal and constitutional principles. But underlying the case—inspiring the plaintiffs to challenge the law and explaining why the decision alternately delighted and horrified many Americans—are powerful ideas and practices that underlie and also go beyond what the Second Amendment does or doesn't mean. They have to do with self-defense and self-identity, and they aren't so much about the Constitution or empirical reality as they are about a wider and deeper cultural war.

4. Gun Stories, Gun Culture, and Gun Prejudice

It's a common trope in books about guns or gun control to begin with a tightly told, evocative story of something very, very bad that happened because someone had a gun. (An alternate take on this genre is the "very bad thing that happened because someone *didn't* have a gun" story.) These stories work, at least for the reader they are designed for, because such stories are true. Bad things do happen with a gun as the tool; bad things are prevented because a gun was available to be used as a tool; mothers weep because the wrong person had a gun and used it to do evil; men grit their teeth and lose their dignity because they didn't have a gun at a moment when one was needed.

True narratives capture readers' attention and make them feel the implications of what they're being told must be true, because the stories are rooted in fact. These stories are never told just for their inherent narrative drive, merely for the art of the reporter capturing a dark moment in the human story. Instead, they are always told to imply something larger about what ought to be done when it comes to gun policy in America. Many such stories are out there: troubled men (pretty much always) who act out their rage by assuming temporary power over others, fearful aftermaths, punishing loss. And then there's the other kind of story, with less outer drama, but plenty internal: men and women who stand up for their own and others' lives with a grim and dangerous, but sometimes necessary, tool.

Far more details tend to be available to the typical researcher or reader about the tragedies, the innocents murdered with impunity because *the wrong person had a gun.* "Wrong person" is the right term. A lot of gun regulation is based on trying to identify that "wrong person." Of course, such laws do far more than they have to do if their goal is keeping us safe from those who would use guns to harm innocents. Even in the most frightening-sounding

71

categories of people forbidden to buy guns by the 1968 Gun Control Act—"felons" or "those adjudicated mentally defective"—far more of them would own or use guns in a peaceful fashion than would misuse them. But that would never make the evening news—never be a juicy anecdote for reportage on the evils of America's gun obsession.

Every day in my e-mail inbox, I get numerous stories of people who have prevented someone from harming them—stealing from them, injuring them—with the judicious and (hopefully) legal use of a weapon. But that's because I'm looking for those stories. I subscribe to an every-weekday newsfeed designed for libertarians called "Rational Review News." In the most recent month, that feed had 25 such stories. They were legitimately reported on news sites or in newspapers but were not the sort that ever become (not that they should) American legends or the source of terms that evoke fear, disgust, and existential horror like "Columbine" or "Virginia Tech."

But if you aren't looking for such stories, you are not apt to come across them. The story of guns in America is written overwhelmingly in the blood of innocent victims if you get it from the front pages or the evening news. As I write this book in August 2008, the main headlines on MSN.com's homepage contain a story about a disgruntled worker in a book warehouse shooting two former colleagues in Bristol, Pennsylvania. The daily stories of gun self-defense that get reported in the generally small local news sources I see in the Rational Review feed will never make MSN headlines.

Osha Grey Davidson's 1993 book on the NRA's history and lobbying power, *Under Fire*, begins with a gripping extended 17-page narrative of the 1989 Stockton, California, schoolyard massacre. He explores the minds of a violent criminal and of his terrified victims. This is how Davidson chose to frame and introduce a book on the history and influence of what is, whether you support its goal or not, essentially a civil rights lobby. What Davidson is trying to say is that the civil right that the NRA defends, the one protected by the Second Amendment, is nothing but a front for the most vicious of crimes. Little wonder gun-rights supporters often feel embattled and suspect their opponents don't respect the innocent decisions they make about how to protect themselves, amuse themselves, or fulfill themselves.

To be sure, without guns, no one could send projectiles at high speed through 33 people in a handful of minutes. But what if there were not fewer guns at the scene of these crimes, but *more*? Nothing earns more sneering contempt—with less evidence—from gun-control advocates than maintaining that in certain situations, a gun-caused horror would have been *less* horrible with *more* guns. Rebecca Peters, head of the International Action Network on Small Arms (which advocates complete worldwide civilian disarmament), once told the NRA's Wayne LaPierre in a debate that lawful self-defense of that variety "only happens in the movies."

But it stands to reason that a skilled gun-wielding innocent can stop a gun-wielding criminal. And it has happened. At least two school mass shootings were brought to a halt by the impossible, Hollywood, Dirty Harry expedient of an armed citizen behaving heroically. For example, in 1997 in Pearl, Mississippi, an angry 16-year-old killed two and wounded seven with a lever-action rifle that had to be reloaded after every shot. Having kept his Colt .45 and bullets stored, as per law, outside the school building and in his truck, assistant principal Joel Myrick ran for it and was able to confront and stop the killer as he was getting ready to drive away, zip to another school, and kill more before the cops arrived.

Had Myrick been able to have his weapon at hand, lives might have been saved or injuries prevented. Yet Myrick later reported that even in his own school, most of his colleagues seemed uncomfortable with what he'd done—unwilling to censure him, but unwilling to support him either. Most press accounts of the event failed to mention that a citizen with a gun stopped the shooter, letting readers assume that police had stopped the killing.

In a similar instance, in 1998 in Edinboro, Pennsylvania, a local teen killed one and wounded three. Local merchant James Strand pointed a shotgun at the teenager while he was reloading and got him to surrender. Media coverage of this incident also overwhelmingly neglected to mention the role of the armed citizen in halting the crime.

At their best, when courts, scholars, journalists, advocates, and politicians think about guns and gun rights, their analysis is based on a wide and sophisticated understanding of the relevant data, the constitutional and legal history, and the social science studies, using wise judgments on what is and is not relevant. But the best isn't always so. And it isn't only policy, academic, or judicial elites whose thoughts and judgments about guns and gun laws matter: it's the electorate, both at large and in the organized pressure groups on both sides of the gun debate, whose passions help guide legislators and, undoubtedly, the courts as well. Even in the recent past, the five justices would not likely have felt emboldened to decide *Heller* as they did, despite their intellectual predilections. It was unlikely that the case would have been heard by the Supreme Court at all. Then came the academic revolution in favor of the individual rights interpretation, the spread and seeming success of concealed carry laws, and some electoral turnarounds against gun regulators since their halcyon days of the Brady Bill and the assault weapons ban.

Both mass public and elite opinion about the role guns play in America are fed in important ways by the popular media, fiction and nonfiction. And the picture the media presents is off-kilter, poorly framed, and obscured with spattered blood. This issue has been analyzed by criminologist Gary Kleck, who has noted in his 2001 book *Armed* (co-authored with Don Kates) a variety of modes of bias against guns and gun owners, including deliberately evading facts that make a vague scary story seem less scary. Kleck cited several examples: news video showing machine guns firing when the topic is semiautomatic weapons, which fire only one bullet per trigger pull; stories about the threat of armor-piercing ammunition, the so-called cop killer bullet, which failed to note that not a single documented case existed in which such a bullet had killed a police officer; and a 1989 story attempting to intimate a tragic and growing pattern of children dying in gun accidents that didn't mention, though Kleck was interviewed by the reporter and told her, that nationally, fatal gun accidents involving children had fallen from 227 in 1974 to 92 in 1987.

When it comes to assessing the politics of gun control, Kleck also noted that trivial and largely meaningless pro-gun-control victories get huge play. His examples were banning the nonexistent "plastic" gun, the "cop killer" ammo ban, and the assault weapons ban— each of almost zero criminological significance. Conversely, the 1980s trend of NRA victories in getting state governments to pass statewide laws that pre-empt local gun regulations—23 such laws passed from 1982 to 1987—was mostly ignored.

Major media, when it comes to guns, will simply *make things up* to create a scary headline. An October 14, 1985, *Newsweek* story trying to gin up a machine gun crisis claimed on the cover that

74

500,000 automatic weapons were haunting America. But that figure was (1) a pure guess and (2) actually pertained to semiautomatic weapons, not automatic machine guns. *Newsweek*'s competitor *Time* in 1989 sent form letters to readers who complained about bias in its gun coverage by blatantly noting, "The time for opinions on the dangers of gun availability is long since gone, replaced by overwhelming evidence that it represents a growing threat to public safety."

The *Washington Post* famously (at least to the gun-rights community) ran editorials in favor of gun control for 77 straight days in 1965. The *New York Times* has found room to report on academic studies that seem to indicate concealed carry laws have not done much to lessen crime and ignores studies that indicate otherwise. In general, if your information and attitudes about guns were formed mostly by normal media channels and you were not personally enmeshed in gun culture, your image of the value of and the problems associated with guns would be the sort that might make a D.C.-level gun ban seem to make sense.

While multiple-victim shootings get heavily reported *because* they are rare, memories of such stories can lead people to assume that we are living in an impossibly violent and tragic world and that guns are its master and its demon. That disjoint between gun reality and gun fears was also, strangely, the theme of the most popular and widely seen anti-gun propaganda of the past decade: left-wing documentarian Michael Moore's 2002 hit, the Oscar-winning *Bowling for Columbine*.

The movie was rightly criticized (for example, by Second Amendment scholar David T. Hardy) for being misleading, and deliberately so, in many of its details. Considering how the debate about guns has shifted in a pro-gun direction lately, it is interesting that even Moore did not argue that the Second Amendment does not protect a right to private possession of guns. On camera, disingenuously or not, he agreed it *does* guarantee such a right. Nor did he blindly assume that the *presence* of guns equals problems with gun violence, as witness his exploration of a Canada that was also relatively filled with guns and relatively lacking in gun violence.

Moore's movie did an interesting, if confusing, little postmodern turnaround on his own implicit point. He argued that the *reason* Americans want to own so many guns (which can lead, in the wrong hands, to tragedies, which he detailed at great length, such as Columbine and the shooting of one six-year-old by another in Flint, Michigan) is that they are made needlessly afraid by the media emphasis on crime and violence. He said this in a documentary that is itself built entirely on making too much of the larger significance of a couple of tragic, but very rare, incidents. He did not, for example, tell his viewers that annual firearm deaths had plummeted around 40 percent in America in the decade prior to making his movie.

Moore would rather mock than rely on facts or even well-developed arguments. The only characters in *Bowling for Columbine* who made sensible points about the responsibility, both civic and personal, to be prepared to use weapons skillfully when necessary were members of the Michigan Militia. And they were meant to be laughable in their pretensions and threatening in their connection (in his movie, at least) with convicted Oklahoma City bombing accomplice Terry Nichols's brother, James Nichols.

Guns are useful tools against those who would harm us. That much is evident from the fact that we all, with nearly universal agreement, arm our paid civic defenders, the police, with guns. Many gun-control advocates seem to assume, and sometimes state outright, that we as individuals don't need to have these dangerous weapons to protect ourselves, our homes, or our families: we have *professional police* for that.

This is so obviously untrue that it's hard to imagine anyone believes it independently of an aversion to guns that goes beyond empiricism and reason. Any time that you actually need a gun to defend yourself—whether on the streets or in your home—a policeman will almost certainly not be there. And precedent after precedent has declared that the police have no legal obligation whatsoever to provide protection for you—even when, as in D.C., the government robs you of your means of protecting yourself.

Even if you had a phone to summon the police instantly when a threatening intruder walked through your broken window, to use D.C. as an example, the average wait time for a police response to an emergency call in the year that *Parker* was filed was 8 minutes and 25 seconds. The great majority of actively life-threatening interactions between a criminal and an unarmed victim would be over long before then.

The anti-gun-control essayist Jeff Snyder, in his book *Nation of Cowards*, makes a vivid and strong anti-empirical case for gun liberty.

76

He surveyed the two leading scientific studies on either side of the debate about whether guns tend to be a social good, those by Arthur Kellerman and Gary Kleck. He concluded that "asserting that Kleck's statistics justify owning or carrying a gun commits the same error as asserting that Kellerman's statistics justify not owning or banning guns. *Both treat the gun as an agent, with independent power to affect results.* In both cases, the gun has become a force, like a chemical, a drug or microbe, with independent power to cause results apart from our decisions, our character and purpose."

Snyder is uncompromising, as he thinks any human should be when it comes to life and safety. As he wrote in the *Washington Times* in 1994, any American with self-respect or a decent regard for his own life or that of his loved ones "must carry arms. Everywhere and at all times." Statistical risk, "safe" neighborhoods be damned. If your life is worth anything, it is worth protecting at all times and in all places, not just occasionally or in the home. "We ... do not live at the pleasure and discretion of the lawless," he said. Snyder hearkens back to a type of person and type of culture that we may have lost, on the large scale, many years ago.

America's political classes don't share Snyder's vigorous self-reliance. Horrible scenes of cowardly criminals wreaking destruction, claiming godlike power over innocent victims, don't tend to inspire us to make sure that we—who can use weapons with wisdom and probity—are better armed and better trained. We don't as a polity seem to encourage each other to take direct responsibility for the strange and threatening things that can and do happen in the world (though still very rarely).

The Stockton, California, shooting of 33 school children and school personnel by a man with semiautomatic weapons in 1989 didn't lead to a wave of support for wider freedom to carry weapons, even in "gun free zones" like schools; it led instead to the assault weapons ban. Even a supposed NRA pawn like George H. W. Bush declared he'd be happy with a ban on the weapon that the killer used.

Self-defense, to many, is morally atavistic, barbaric, and just plain wrong. The Snyders of the world would sneer at attempts to argue for self-defense on "social good" grounds. His defense of self-defense is not based on a larger social good. To him it is an individual right, an individual responsibility, that everyone is obligated to take upon themselves.

Most of those who advocate armed self-defense believe that a culture wherein more people have the means and will to defend themselves, their families, and their homes is likely to be one in which criminals are less bold and less active. A popular epigram for the gun-rights community, from science fiction writer Robert Heinlein, was alluded to by Dick Heller himself on the steps of the Supreme Court, right after the *Heller* hearings: "An armed society is a polite society."

That may not be an unshakeable rule—certain cultures might break down to a mutually ugly war given widespread gun carrying. But even in such cultures of honor where, as southern writer Harry Crews put it, a blood insult demands blood, a code exists that at least reminds people they can't treat other people as playthings for careless pleasure or whim. Certain disciplines are demanded and the rest of the social world has a will of its own.

Pro-gun-regulation author Robert Spitzer has said explicitly that any feelings of safety that might result from owning guns—and by implication actually *being* safer—should be overwhelmed by concerns about public welfare and public morality. "Public" health, the "social" effects—this is the very language of the scientists and activists who argue for stronger gun regulations. Individuals who, like a Tom Palmer or a Shelly Parker, might live or die based on their ability to have and use weapons are expendable in pursuit of the larger social goal. This divide beween the "public" and the "individual" good is why compromise on gun regulation is so difficult to come by.

Threaded through the political fight over gun control is a cultural fight and a feeling of danger on both sides. The regulators think the nonregulators are a hair's breadth away from unleashing murderous public mayhem or at least killing themselves or their loved ones in a moment of weakness. The nonregulators think the regulators are itching to take from them their best means to preserve their own lives. And both think that the other side is full of people who simply do not mean well and cannot be trusted.

Accusations of rank hypocrisy are often thrown at—and often earned by—some of the more earnest gun opponents. Sarah Brady, wife of wounded anti-gun icon James Brady, herself bought a gun for her son. Public opponents of guns from Rosie O'Donnell to *New York Times* publisher Arthur Sulzberger Jr. question the need for anyone to have guns, yet either have guns themselves or pay professionals with guns to protect them.

Owning a gun does not make you an eccentric in America. Far from it. Forty to fifty percent of American households have guns. In over two dozen states, open carrying of a weapon you legally own is perfectly legal, often without even a permit required. Still, publicly standing up for the value of gun possession and gun carrying can get you mocked.

In the small "open carry" movement, gun owners encourage each other to carry their weapons publicly. By walking about, harmlessly strapped in public, they want to demonstrate that guns have a place in civilized society—that it is not guns, but careless or evil gun users, that cause problems. According to media coverage of the open-carry phenomenon, these individuals are at best thought of as annoying eccentrics, and they are at worst fit to have the cops called on them— even though what they are doing is perfectly legal in the relevant municipalities and states.

As I worked on this book, I met lots of people who love guns in lots of ways. I learned that in any social gathering of more than five Americans, if I mentioned I was working on a book involving guns and gun rights, someone would pipe in with an either first- or second-hand story about someone deeply involved in guns. Occasionally the stories were tragic—a disturbed cousin shooting an aunt. Even I could add a story: an acquaintance of mine, the wife of an old friend, was herself killed in a freak recreational shooting accident. Often the stories were more amusing, though sometimes indicating obsessions—the uncle with dozens of weapons who bought lots of acreage in Nevada just so he could shoot freely or the former policeman dad with complicated thoughts about gun control. All of us, even those of us who don't own or think of them often, are close to guns in this country.

Consider a couple of examples. Matt Hughes is an unusual man in some ways. He's a nine-time UFC (Ultimate Fighting Championship, a mixed martial arts competition) welterweight champion and author of a *New York Times* best-selling autobiography. But in his demeanor, honesty, politeness, and aggressive Midwest normality, he's classically, and commonly, American. When I mentioned I was working on this book to our mutual friend Michael Malice (co-author of Hughes's autobiography), Malice said, "Wow, if you want to talk about guns in America, talk to Matt."

Hughes didn't seem to agree that his interest in guns was worthy of much storytelling or analysis. He just likes them, enjoys target shooting (often with his eight-year-old son alongside) on his huge estate in rural Illinois, and owns, he's pretty sure, over 100 of them, though he hasn't counted. But when I pressed him about the politics of guns—something he's lucky enough not to have to think about much—he realized that, yes, he *can* get political when he thinks about people wanting to overly regulate or prohibit his free use of these devices that mean both pleasure and protection to him and his family. He even admitted, "To be real honest, if something came along and the government wanted to take my guns, I don't know how I'd feel about that. The government taking guns away from American citizens? The government might want to watch out about a revolt. If the government wanted to see if they could have one, that would be a way to do it. I don't wanna give my guns up, and I don't think I have to. I don't know. It's one of those questions I'd have to answer when I came to it. I might be one of the guys who might think it's a decent cause worth dying for, the right to bear arms."

Hughes's gun use is very normal, though the number of guns he has is unusual. (Owning multiple weapons—the proverbial "arsenal" that gun controllers often complain about—is common among gun owners; around three-fourths of households who own any guns own two or more.) He enjoys shooting on his property with his family.

I also talked to a man named Joe Huffman about his use of guns. Hoffman is more unusual in his dedication to the shooting arts. He runs a yearly event called Boomershoot in Idaho, at which people shoot hundreds of yards at four-inch square targets to set off high explosives.

It's wild fun, of course—an intense experience most shooters don't get to have. It attracts a lot of media attention for that reason. Like Hughes, when I pressed Huffman on the subject, he explained that more than just pleasure and amusement lies at the heart of his gun ownership. He thinks it's important to cultivate arcane, high-skilled shooting arts in people he knows because a time may come, as the Founding Fathers knew, when such skills might be useful for more than just outré amusement.

Few advocates of severe gun regulation publicly stake out a position the direct opposite of pro-gun essayist Jeff Snyder's. That is,

80

few would claim it doesn't matter what the social science facts say about who is or isn't harmed by guns, guns are simply *bad things* and having them in private hands is just *wrong*; that any tragedy caused by guns is sufficient to damn the objects; that the tears of anyone who has lost a loved one due to violence facilitated by a gun should drown out any talk of dignity, the right to self-defense, or any research indicating that guns might be a net positive.

Still, when gun-control advocates let their hair down regarding their assumptions about liberty, dignity, and character which underlie their desire to disarm the country, neither appeals to the virtues of self-reliance and self-defense nor empirical evidence (for more on this see chapter 5) on how guns tend to be used seems to matter much. Harvard School of Public Health Professor Deborah Prothrow-Stith, who studies the subject, admitted, "I hate guns, and I cannot imagine why anyone would want to own one."

That sentiment seems echoed by the epigram chosen for the 1994 anti-gun book *Lethal Passage: How the Travels of a Single Handgun Expose the Roots of America's Gun Crisis* by Erik Larson. It's from D. H. Lawrence: "The essential American soul is hard, isolate, stoic, and a killer." How could we countenance allowing a people with that kind of essential soul to have free access to tools of death and destruction? Gun dealers, to Larson, are not people trying to meet a widespread human need, surrounded on all sides by complicated and hard-to-follow regulations—which they are sometimes entrapped into breaking. They are knowing accomplices to murder, full stop.

Many Americans find they cannot be emotionally detached when it comes to guns. So many guns are in America, we are all close to instances of their use or misuse. I have not myself been a gun enthusiast, though I've gone shooting both in ranges and out in the desert a handful of times with friends who are. I've even participated in fun-dangerous activities like shooting at far-off propane canisters. As a journalist, and a libertarian advocate, I have cared about guns and gun rights as a public policy matter. But gun rights is one of the trickiest and most difficult of traditional American liberties to stand up for. Make no mistake, many people in America believe that openly advocating relatively unrestricted liberty to own and use weapons marks you as a dangerous Neanderthal and an enemy of the Republic.

Conversely, in many parts of America, thinking that guns are bad and dangerous and that it's wrong to allow so many people to have them marks you as beyond the pale of respectable citizenry, a quisling to the American revolution, a disgusting half-human unwilling or unable to bear the necessary burdens of both citizenship and basic humanity.

Between these two types of people, the debate about gun policy can never be a bloodless matter of constitutional interpretation or criminological data. A gap of values and culture and interpretation yawns, one that's well-nigh unbridgeable. The *Heller* decision will not change that.

The *Heller* case could have ended with the D.C. Circuit Court of Appeals victory for Levy's team. Elements in the gun-control movement, though none would admit it on the record, were begging D.C. Mayor Adrian Fenty to "take one for the team," to *not* appeal his city's legal defeat to the Supreme Court. If Fenty let his loss stand, the Supreme Court would have no opportunity to set a precedent that could damage the gun-control cause nationally. D.C. could just make cosmetic adjustments to its gun regulations and see what happened. Levy's team hoped Fenty would keep fighting. An appeals court victory was nice, but they had their eyes on a bigger prize: a victory in the Supreme Court.

Levy wrote an op-ed in the *Washington Post* more or less goading Fenty into taking the case all the way. The District of Columbia seemed hesitant. But after getting an extension, D.C. finally decided, on September 4, 2007, to petition the Supreme Court for certiorari. On November 20, 2007, the Court agreed to take the case. What had been *Parker v. District of Columbia* and was now *District of Columbia v. Heller* had made it to the highest court in the land.

Surprisingly, the NRA was still threatening the case's progress. A law can only be challenged for violating a constitutional right if that law is still in effect. An NRA-supported bill, known as the District of Columbia Personal Protection Act, was moving through Congress. The bill would essentially repeal all the constitutionally objectionable gun laws in D.C. Levy and his team had had their eyes on the bill's progress for some time; Levy had even testified against it before Congress in June 2005. Although he agreed with the policy objective of the bill, if it passed it would kill the chance to establish a landmark precedent in the Supreme Court. That this bill was still a live option, Levy's team thought, was another NRA attempt to knock its case off the rails. A casual observer might have seen the NRA doing its thing, standing up for the rights of D.C. gun owners in a way that would, just coincidentally, make moot an ongoing Supreme Court challenge. But what difference would that make, the law would be gone anyway, right?

However, if DCPPA passed, not only would the *Heller* case go away but the positive, individual-rights affirming decision from Silberman in the appellate court would essentially be wiped off the record book as well. And unlike a positive Supreme Court decision, the DCPPA was no permanent solution. It could easily be reversed by a future Congress; and it would affect only D.C., establishing no usable precedent anywhere else.

The Levy team went into overdrive, meeting with senators and representatives to convince them that, yes, we all shared the same goal—the overthrow of D.C.'s gun ban—but that the legal route through the Supreme Court was a better path to that goal. It was more meaningful and effective, not just for D.C. but for establishing a useful precedent for the whole country.

"We were outraged," Neily recalled, "and had a meeting with NRA higher ups and they told us, 'We've done this many times before. We've pushed this legislation often. Don't worry, we're just going through the motions since our membership expects us to do it. If it looks like it's going to pass, we'll pull the plug on it, don't worry.' I didn't believe that for a minute; I think they were absolutely serious [about the DCPPA]. This was from an organization that had already tried to derail our case twice." In their lobbying efforts, Neily recalled, "We got commitments [to not let the legislation through] from enough high-level people in the Congress who said it with enough conviction we thought they meant it."

"We succeeded," Levy said. "Or more precisely, their effort failed—I'm sure it wasn't just because we lobbied against it. For whatever reason, Congress decided they weren't going to deal with it, so the D.C. law still existed and our case went forward."

That was the end of NRA efforts to frustrate the case. When various parties supporting the case gathered at the Heritage Foundation to coordinate and plan duties in writing amicus briefs for *Heller* in September 2007, Neily recalled, the NRA was "fully responsive and fully cooperative at that point. I understand some of their reasons for resisting our effort. They would have done themselves a favor if they had taken a different approach, but I don't have particular ill will."

"Now they have become our allies," Levy said the week of the March 2008 Supreme Court hearing. "And they are formidable allies, and we are most happy to have their support." He pointed to the amicus brief the NRA helped assemble, one written by Stephen Halbrook, signed by *the majority* of Congress—250 representatives, 55 senators, and Vice President Dick Cheney—as one very appealing fruit of the NRA's born-again support for *Heller*.

Chris Cox, head of the NRA's Institute for Legislative Action, was also happy with how his organization's relationship to *Heller* turned out. Sure, there was conflict along the way, he admitted. "In my experience, you get a bunch of lawyers in the room and you'll probably not have agreement," he said. "There was concern prior to Roberts and Alito even being on the Court as to whether or not the timing was right. It all worked out. Was it lucky? Was it strategy? I'll let other people answer that. A lot of things played into this case. But I applaud Alan and his team. The victory was ultimately due to a lot of hard work by a lot of people for decades, certainly including the NRA, and in the end the Second Amendment is stronger."

The NRA was now a good friend. And the case needed dozens of other good friends as the often fractious world of scholars and interest groups wanting to vindicate the Second Amendment circled the wagons to move *Heller* through potentially hostile territory to the promised land: a Supreme Court decision that would say the Second Amendment guarantees an individual right.

The *Heller* fight couldn't rely on purely historical, legal, or linguistic analysis. D.C. was arguing that its regulations were reasonable ways to achieve a legitimate public purpose. Thus, questions about what purpose gun control really serves, and whether D.C.'s regulations were in fact meeting such purposes, would come into play. The Court, and certainly the court of public opinion, would likely have to grapple as well with questions about the empirical realities of gun policy in D.C. and in America.

5. Guns by Numbers and *Heller*'s Day in Court

People passionate about gun culture—either for or against—are a minority. To most people, the most sensible policy toward guns—what rights to own, use, and sell weapons we should recognize—is best decided by examining empirical reality, not value judgments about violence, risk, and self-reliance.

Thus, the debate about guns and gun control has been fought not just in courts and not only with constitutional interpretation as a weapon. When D.C.'s Mayor Fenty defended his city's gun policies, and later lamented their death, he stressed over and over again that laws prohibiting ownership of guns made the people of D.C. safer.

Was Fenty right? On examining the record of D.C.'s violent crime and murder rates since 1976, in comparison with its own past and with the rest of America and similarly sized cities, it doesn't look like it. Indeed, in 2003, D.C.'s murder rate was worse than Baghdad's, as noted in a *Heller* amicus brief from "Criminologists, Social Scientists, Other Distinguished Scholars, and the Claremont Institute," written by gun scholar Don Kates.

In their filings, Fenty and his *amici* relied almost entirely on one study for its claim that D.C.'s gun laws had saved lives. The study, by Colin Loftin, published in the 1991 *New England Journal of Medicine*, purported to show that D.C.'s gun ban had indeed lowered homicides in D.C. The study is not sturdy enough to support all the weight Fenty placed on it. In the first place, it stops at 1987. In the second place, it takes advantage of the District's huge drops in population and concomitant drop in whole numbers of murders and violent crimes (even though the rates per capita rose enormously) to claim that lives have been saved. A critique of Loftin's study in the aforementioned *Heller* amicus brief from criminologists and sociologists found that if you adjusted the spans of years he used for his comparison even one year in either direction, all his supposed benefits disappeared—a sign of cherry picking for the best possible results, not objective research.

Besides, rates per 100,000 population are a far more meaningful measure of safety. If half the city fled its out-of-control violence, of course you'd expect to find a smaller number of crimes and murder victims. But using the rate-per-population measure shows D.C. violent crime and murder rates have become far *worse* since D.C. passed its supposedly crime-stopping and life-saving laws. A D.C. with defensive gun use outlawed has not been a safer D.C.

Every year but one since 1976, the murder rate per 100,000 has exceeded that in 1976. In 10 of the 30 years after 1976, the rate has been more than twice as high. One of the best years for D.C. to put forward to argue that its gun laws did any good was 2006. With a rate that year of 29.1 murders per 100,000, it was D.C.'s best year since 1985. Even so, D.C.'s murder rate in 2006 was five times the national average and more than double the rate in comparably sized urban areas. And the percentage of D.C. homicides committed with guns—generally around 80 percent—is also higher than the national average, despite their ban.

Some more context is useful. Maryland and Virginia—the neighbors D.C. tends to blame for its murder problem because guns are still legal there—have had significantly lower murder rates (both before and after D.C.'s gun ban). Before the 1976 ban, D.C.'s murder rate tended to float around three times that of its neighboring states. That trend continued until the mid-1980s, at which point D.C.'s rate, with its supposedly public-safety-enhancing gun ban, leapt to between seven and eight times the murder rate in Maryland and Virginia and stayed that high in comparison for well over a decade.

Maryland and Virginia have fairly large rural portions, so a comparison with other large urban areas might be more apt. Again, there is no evidence of D.C.'s gun ban increasing public safety. Before the 1976 ban, D.C.'s murder rate compared with the 49 other largest cities varied widely. It was the same in some cases and as much as 50 percent higher in others. By the early 1990s, after 15 years of a gun ban, D.C.'s murder rate rose to three or more times as high as those other cities and stayed there throughout the decade.

Fenty might imagine that without his city's gun laws the situation would be even worse. But there's every reason to believe that when criminals know the law-abiding are almost certainly not armed, they are emboldened toward more crime and violence.

Both those who agree with 19th-century Supreme Court Justice Joseph Story that the right to own weapons is the "palladium of liberty" and those who believe that guns are evil fall back on what they can assert is cold, hard empirical reality to buttress their policy stance. Yet cross-cultural comparisons show no reliable correlation between presence of guns and violent crime. The same applies within the United States as well. As criminologist Gary Kleck explained in a 1990 address to the National Academy of Sciences/National Research Council Panel on the Understanding and Prevention of Violence: "The best currently available evidence, imperfect though it is (and must always be), indicates that general gun availability has no measurable net positive effect on rates of homicide, suicide, robbery, assault, rape, or burglary in the United States. This is not the same as saying gun availability has no effects on violence—it has many effects on the likelihood of attack, injury, death, and crime completion, but these effects work in both violence-increasing and violence-decreasing directions, with the effects largely canceling out. For example, when aggressors have guns, they are (1) *less* likely to physically attack their victims, (2) *less* likely to injure the victim given an attack, but (3) *more* likely to kill the victim, given an injury. Further, when *victims* have guns, it is less likely aggressors will attack or injure them and less likely they will lose property in a robbery. At the aggregate level, in both the best available time series and cross-sectional studies, the overall net effect of gun availability on total rates of violence is not significantly different from zero."

And in 2004 when the National Academy of Sciences reviewed 253 journal articles, 99 books, and 43 government publications, evaluating 80 gun-control measures, the researchers concluded that "existing research studies . . . do not credibly demonstrate a causal relationship between the ownership of firearms and the cause or prevention of criminal violence or suicide."

A year earlier, the Centers for Disease Control and Prevention reported on an independent evaluation of firearms and ammunition bans, restrictions on acquisition, waiting periods, registration, licensing, child-access prevention laws, and zero-tolerance laws. The conclusion was this: there is "insufficient evidence to determine the effectiveness of any of the firearms laws or combinations of laws reviewed on violent outcomes."

Gun controllers rely on a small number of supposed gold-standard academic studies to buttress their belief that gun laws are definitely good for public safety. They deny, on the individual level, that having your own gun in the home will make you safer. This has become one of those well-understood "facts," even among people who admit they don't follow the gun debate closely: having a gun in the home is far more likely to harm you than to help you.

The most-relied-on source of that belief in the past decade or so is the research of Dr. Arthur Kellerman as published in the *New England Journal of Medicine* in a 1993 article, "Gun Ownership as a Risk Factor for Homicide in the Home." Kellerman's influence was huge and immediate; within two months of the journal article appearing, it had been mentioned or cited in print and on the air more than 100 times. Kellerman's essential argument was this: for every time a gun is used in the home for self-defense, there are multiple instances when a gun in the home leads to accidents, crimes, or suicides. Even if that's true, it's irrelevant. The benefit of a gun in the home is not to shoot bad guys. That rarely happens. The real benefit is the deterrent effect on the commission of crimes—countless instances of violent acts *not* undertaken because the potential victims might be able to defend themselves with suitable firearms.

While Kellerman found many examples of home homicides, Gary Kleck found that Kellerman "did not document a single case in which the victim was killed with a gun kept in the victim's home." Overwhelmingly, the killer *brought* the gun into the home. Kleck further found that many other factors Kellerman identified about his study group were far more strongly associated with being murdered than owning a gun—for example, drinking problems, living alone, and being a renter. It has not yet become a dimly recalled factoid that renting means you are more likely to be murdered in your home.

The field of gun numerology is a roiling pool of contentions and refutations, and Kellerman's skeptical reflections on the merits of home gun possession have been widely disputed. Daniel Polsby, in an article on gun control in the March 1994 *Atlantic*, points out that Kellerman had a hard time separating out instances where the gun clearly led to the violence, and incidents where violent people, or people in dangerous lines of work, used guns or armed themselves because they knew violence was likely in their lives.

Even Kellerman admitted in his study, "It is possible that reverse causation accounted for some of the association we observed between gun ownership and homicide." Polsby notes that from Kellerman's own data, it's equally possible that *most* of the association is from reverse causation: that people living lives where violence was likely or expected tended to have guns, not that having a gun made it more likely they would get killed. For example, people involved in crime themselves, whether mugging, robbery, or drugs, might be more likely to be armed in their homes than the average American and also to attract violence toward their home.

From 1946 to 2004, while per capita gun ownership increased nearly 150 percent in the United States, the murder rate decreased 17 percent. Clearly, guns in and of themselves aren't causing murders. And then guns are blamed for more than just planned or intentional violence. They are also often implicated in completely accidental deaths. But for whatever reason—perhaps wider awareness of the need for care in dealing with dangerous weapons—even as per capita gun ownership has increased greatly, accidental gun deaths have fallen greatly. From 1948 to 2004, per capita gun ownership in America increased from 0.36 guns per person to nearly 1.0. During that same period, fatal gun accidents per capita decreased enormously, from 1.60 per 100,000 to only 0.22 per 100,000. More guns certainly don't equal more accidental gun deaths.

This is a public policy debate in which the right to dignity and self-defense are generally not enough to settle anything—and in which most people would place "empirical facts" over constitutional rights. One of the most contentious empirical questions can be framed this way: you gun-rights advocates say that guns are *not* just machines of death and evil—not just tools that criminals and the angry use to murder, that innocents use to cause accidental deaths, and that the confused use for suicide—but are useful tools to the innocent in deterring or stopping killers, rapists, and robbers. If that's so, exactly *how* useful are they? This question is at the heart of one of the empirical debates most angrily contended and refuted in the gun conversation, known as the "defensive gun use" or "DGU" question. Unfortunately, the answer to the question "how often are guns used defensively by innocents in America?" is "no one really knows."

That does not mean we don't have some suggestive study results that indicate possible magnitudes. Still, contemplating the attempts to answer the DGU question from both sides gives interesting support to Jeff Snyder's argument that science and numbers can't give authoritative, value-free answers to our policy and ethical questions regarding guns.

The opposing armies in the DGU war are roughly staked out with these dueling positions: (1) there are a really large number of DGUs, so many that any reasonable person would have to admit that private gun ownership is some kind of social good; and (2) while there may be a fair number of DGUs, the number is dwarfed by the number of violent crimes committed with guns. So never mind the people who save themselves with guns, politicians should concentrate on the crimes and loss of life and limb that we can see accompany gun possession and use.

Left out of any policy decision based on these sorts of macrostatistics, as always, is how much having a gun mattered to the specific individual person able to defend himself. That's another reason it was important that the *Heller* debate could be hooked on specific human beings and their stories, not merely social scientist debates.

Gary Kleck did the research most relied on by gun-rights supporters to indicate a large number of DGUs. Kleck's data comes from a spring 1993 set of telephone surveys, asking people about their experiences with defensive use of guns in the home. The survey came up with a (controversial) estimate of 2.2 to 2.5 million DGUs a year. That sounds big, but as Kleck points out, it amounts to around 1 percent of the guns in America being so used in a year. A later series of telephone surveys by various other researchers exploring the same question found figures within the same ballpark. "Use" does not have to mean actually *firing* the gun—brandishing or announcing its presence, as plaintiff Tom Palmer did, is sufficient. The notion that career criminals, who break into homes, mug, or are involved in illicit business transactions, are more likely to have to use guns is supported by these facts from Kleck's surveys: 99 percent of the gun-owning populace had no examples of DGUs, but nearly a third of households that had experienced a DGU had been involved in more than one such incident. Criminals, as Kleck pointed out, run a higher risk of being criminally attacked than most of us.

The most prominently cited counter to Kleck's data, with numbers that come in far lower than his estimates, is the National Crime Victimization Survey, done by Department of Justice employees, which found from 1992–2005 roughly 97,000 DGUs per year. Kleck cast doubt on these data for various reasons. He doubted that non-anonymous surveyed citizens would accurately admit committing what could be an unlawful act to a government employee. He also noted that the surveyed were never *directly* asked about DGUs. They were asked if they admitted to being a crime victim. Those who answered "yes" were then asked if they tried to do "anything" about the incident while in progress. Also, when asked about the crime victimization experience, the surveyed had already talked about where the crime occurred. Kleck believed this further increased the chance they would be reluctant to confess to a crime, since DGUs outside the home are often far more legally problematic. Kleck also speculated that since a DGU might foil the crime, the surveyed might not even consider the DGU incident a crime committed against them if the crime was attempted but not completed— thus the survey would never find the DGU.

Many of Kleck's opponents similarly assume that lots of people must have lied to him as well, though they don't have as convincing a set of reasons why that might be the case. The strongest objection to Kleck is that the number of people who claim to have shot and wounded an assailant in his surveys leads to a number of wounded that's higher than reported hospitalized gunshot victims. Kleck presumes that many criminals don't seek medical help, since that would almost certainly lead to talks with cops. And those are conversations that criminals simply don't want to have. The debate is highly polarized. Not surprisingly, people tend to embrace the survey data that suggests the policy prescription they favor.

As already noted, a lot of the gun-control debate doesn't focus much on personal DGUs, but instead on overarching macrostatistics about guns, crime, and violence. Even on that level, it's hard to see any sign that more guns equals more gun crime. Per capita gun ownership has risen pretty steadily in the past 50 or so years (after topping out in 1999 at 0.95, it fell very slightly to 0.93 guns by 2004). This rising presence of guns in America as a whole has corresponded with overall declines in violent crimes in the 1990s; from 1993 to 2006, the firearm crime rate in America decreased by nearly half, from 225 to 129 per 100,000.

Upstanding citizens can and do use guns to defend themselves, almost always without actually having to fire one. The very existence of guns in the civilian population stands as a deterrent to rational criminals, as many surveys of criminals have shown. The spread of guns in the civilian population clearly has no mechanical relation to rising gun crime. The pro-gun-rights position can hold its own not only in the realm of the Constitution and moral reasoning based on the right of self-defense, but in the social sciences.

Among all the numbers, known and estimated, floating around the gun debate, one is little emphasized but well worth remembering: fewer than two-tenths of 1 percent of the extant guns in America will ever be used to commit a crime in any given year; and those will be in the hands of people who have, for a wide variety of reasons, *chosen* to commit a crime—whether in a moment of passion or with long, cool calculation. To use that tiny minority of gun owners' crimes as an excuse, as D.C. tried to do, to force the vast majority of the innocent to have no useful means to defend their lives and dignity should be seen as bad policy even by majoritarians reluctant to privilege individual rights.

In the absence of authoritative data, a lot of "it stands to reason" arguments abound in the gun debate, particularly on the big question of "can gun control work?" Built into that question is the presumption that the goal is known. Gun-rights defenders often darkly assume that the real goal of any niggling bit of regulation (such as laws limiting gun purchases to only one a month) is to keep political momentum going to soften citizens up toward accepting further gun regulations of increasing severity.

Did D.C.'s gun control regulations "work"? If the goal was to make D.C.'s citizens safer, it seems clear that the answer is "no." But the real goal may have simply been to show that D.C.'s government was hanging tough and doing whatever it could, however outrageously excessive and beyond what any other city had ever tried, to try to curb its terrible crime problem.

Parker plaintiff Gillian St. Lawrence understood one reason D.C.'s government might cling tightly to its gun controls despite its failure to cut crime. "The city has a tough time grappling with violence issues," she said. "They have lots of problems that need to be solved, and banning guns is what they tell themselves they can do." In the week before the *Heller* oral arguments, D.C. launched a particularly brazen attempt to reconcile its tough gun laws with its unusually high levels of gun violence, sending cops door to door in bad neighborhoods and asking if they could come in and search for illegal guns. Just asking, you know. They promised not to prosecute just on the gun possession charge. But if the gun turned out to be linked to a known crime, well, watch out.

One of the basic arguments against gun control is that laws regarding possession and sale of guns will just be ignored by the very criminals we should fear being armed, especially if we are not. Like the bumper sticker says: "When guns are outlawed, only outlaws have guns." This argument goes back to colonial times, to the Italian political philosopher Cesare Beccaria. In 1764 he wrote, "the laws which forbid men to bear arms . . . only disarm those who are neither inclined nor determined to commit crimes. Can it be supposed that those who have the courage to violate the most sacred laws of humanity and the most important in the civil code will respect the lesser and more arbitrary laws, which are easier and less risky to break, and which . . . subject the innocent man to all the annoyances which the guilty deserve?"

Some gun-control advocates counter that criminals are often extremely present-oriented, not good long-term planners. If that's so, laying down small barriers in their path, even if they are theoretically surmountable (like most gun laws are) will often be enough to keep a gun from their hands. This is undoubtedly true, in some cases. However, felons are already barred by federal law from obtaining or owning guns in almost all circumstances; still, many of them do get guns, and most of them get their guns in black markets, which in certain states is doubtless far less time-consuming and troublesome than going through the legal market's paperwork, tests, and waiting periods.

The empirical data about the gun-policy debate are often ambiguous, and legitimate arguments about what they mean will continue. When it comes to authoritatively deciding how any given macro fact—presence of guns, state of gun laws—affects another macro fact—numbers of assaults, rapes, murders, or DGUs—law professor Andrew McClurg concluded in a 1999 article in the *Journal on Firearms and Public Policy* that it is "impossible for any statistical study to reliably isolate one causal factor out of hundreds or thousands or millions and say this factor causes violent crime to decline by this amount . . . any attempt to isolate the impact of one causal factor in a situation involving an extremely large number of other possible explanations seems doomed to be fallacious . . . there are simply too many variables contributing to violent crime."

That empirical ambiguity about guns and gun control is still real, and it will continue. But one thing in the gun debate was about to become a settled fact in 2008: what the Second Amendment means in American courts.

Arguing a case before the Supreme Court is serious business. Even the most skilled, experienced, and confident lawyers don't rush in without help from their friends or, in the legal lingo, the *amici*. The *amici* buttress the official briefs from the lawyers with, in this case, dozens of additional briefs making points that the main brief didn't have space for.

The *Heller* team had among its *amici* retired military officers writing on the national security benefits of widespread training on and use of firearms among the populace, that great unorganized militia. Academics for the Second Amendment, in a brief written by scholar David T. Hardy, explained how the ratification debate and sense of the people in the founding era supports the individual right interpretation. The Congress on Racial Equality discussed how blacks have been historically disadvantaged by gun control and are still discriminated against by it today. The Pink Pistols, a gay rights organization, explained how the collective rights interpretation of the Second Amendment discriminates against gays—who because of prejudice and violence aimed against them especially need personal defense and who are not permitted in the standard organized military.

Nearly 20 people prominent in the gun-rights movement gathered at a meeting at the Heritage Foundation in September 2007 to strategize and brainstorm about the *amici* process. No one wanted the Court to get a half dozen briefs parsing *Miller* or explaining the empirical evidence bearing on gun possession and public safety. The idea was to figure out what people or groups would be the strongest advocate with the most knowledge about the focus area for each particular brief. Everyone involved was happy with the set of briefs that resulted.

The linchpins of the process, Neily recalled, were Gura and another lawyer who was not officially part of Heller's team, but who earned a place at the counsel's table during the Supreme Court hearings for all his help and advice: David Kopel of the Independence Institute. "It was not always a smooth process," Neily admitted. "There were disagreements, miscommunication, and frustration. But I've been involved in many of these efforts with [the Institute for Justice], and I was ecstatic with how it ended up, a collection of briefs of excellent quality. Breyer even said so in the oral arguments. The *amici* briefs were an absolutely critical part of this." (Kopel, for his part, credits George Washington University Law Professor Robert Cottrol for his intelligent strategic overview in helping plan and manage the *amici* effort.)

The main *Heller* brief provided a bravura, full-service set of historical, legal, constitutional, and empirical evidence and argument about both the unconstitutionality and lack of wisdom in D.C.'s laws. Gura explained how and why preambles should not, and never have in other contexts, be taken to restrict a plain operative clause; how "keep" and "bear" were by no means exclusively military terms at the time of the amendment's ratification; how all sides of the ratification debate clearly understood the Second Amendment as covering an individual right; and how the militia meant the whole people united in arms, not just a state-organized and run select band.

D.C. for its part tried once again in its Supreme Court brief to sum up the best-case argument against the Second Amendment as an individual right outside the militia and for its gun ban. The City Council made a judgment, which it contended was reasonable for D.C.'s unique purposes and circumstances, that there was no legitimate use for guns in an urban environment. People like Shelly Parker, living among armed criminals who meant her harm, just didn't know their own legitimate needs.

D.C.'s brief also stated—and this would be news to the nearly 8,000 murder victims in D.C. since 1976—that "preventing these harms is not just a legitimate goal; it is a governmental duty of the highest order." It is a duty that D.C. has manifestly failed in— indeed, a duty that does not even exist, according to D.C.'s lawyers when they are responding to lawsuits by victims of the city's failure to protect them from harm.

The City Council's intention, which D.C. claimed protects the constitutionality of its 1976 restriction, was to have "acted to reduce those harms without functionally disarming residents." The District failed at both, but still had its advocates write to the Supreme Court with a straight face that "subsequent evidence supports the Council's judgment that banning handguns saves lives."

A reminder: the per capita murder rate in D.C. has been higher than the year the city passed the ban in every year but one; it has been twice that rate more than 10 years; and the trend is not merely a reflection of national trends for which D.C.'s policies aren't to blame. City officials also tried to rely on the fact D.C. is not technically a state to claim that the Bill of Rights doesn't apply to them anyway—a gambit so bizarre that the Supreme Court ended up ignoring it altogether.

Alan Gura had fought this case through five years of setbacks, frustrations, a steep learning curve, and an appellate victory. *Five years.* He did everything that needed to be done. With Levy's money, the intellectual support of Levy, Healy, and Neily, and against great odds, the team won a clear and total victory at the D.C. Circuit Court of Appeals and got exactly where they wanted to go: The Supreme Court.

Some people in the gun-rights community, which had, by that time, drawn ranks around the case, thought Gura had gone far enough. The boy wonder who had never argued a case before the Supreme Court should step aside—with a distinguished service medal of some sort—and let the big boys take over. Levy, they thought, should hire an experienced Supreme Court advocate, perhaps a Harvard professor or a former solicitor general.

During my interview with Gura a few days after the oral arguments at the Supreme Court, the topic of attempts to replace him animated him like no other. "There is a great deal of professional jealousy in this town," he told me. "A lot of people really believe that they are entitled to do certain things, are privileged by birth to take on certain work. But it is not my purpose in life to advance someone else's career. The idea that I would turn over a business I've developed—and I did develop it, and I want to be very emphatic about this: I designed the litigation. I wrote the pleadings. I designed the strategy. I made the arguments in previous courts. No one knows this case better than I do.

"I had co-counsels, of course; they were helpful and they made contributions. But this is basically something that I've done. Not something I did all by myself, but the primary drafting was mine. Read the briefs and those are my words for the most part, my research, my understanding, my strategy, me, me, me, me, OK?" He's emphatic about this; with some humor—especially those last four me's—but emphatic.

"The idea that I did all this without pay just to turn it over to my masters is absurd. Nobody believed in this when I took it. Doing this type of case was seen as eccentric and kooky. 'Oh, ho ho, the Second Amendment—why not do a Third Amendment case?' That type of crap. But the work product that I put together? I don't believe that anybody else could have done a better job. While I do not doubt certain other lawyers could have done a good job, they wouldn't have done *as* good a job, and certainly no one else was lining up to do this work five years ago."

What really amazed and irked him was that the pressure on Levy to replace him with a more high-profile lawyer with more experience came *after* he had taken it all the way to the Supreme Court.

"I devise this very successful strategy out of nothing," he said wonderingly, "and suddenly I'm incompetent? But in the last 5 to 10 years a group of lawyers in Washington determined it was fantastic marketing to hold themselves out as high priests of the Supreme Court. And when a really nice piece of Supreme Court business comes along and they can't get it, it messes up their market and undercuts the philosophy that only they were special enough. But I didn't get my law degree out of a crackerjack box. I've had real positions of responsibility. I'm not stupid, and even if I am stupid, in *this* case I'm not."

Levy fully agreed. Gura was his man. He'd performed impeccably and had stuck with a *very* poor-paying gig for *much* longer than he thought he'd have to. They had been loyal to each other and were going to stay that way. Besides, Levy didn't believe there was any reason to think twice about letting Gura take the case all the way. "He knows this case better than anyone in the world," Levy told me the week before the Supreme Court hearing, "including anyone the D.C. government could hire. He's very, very well prepared for this case."

The D.C. government may also have been a little nervous about how well-prepared Levy's team was. As Neily said, "It must have been incredibly difficult for a take-charge guy like Fenty" to still be fighting this case at the Supreme Court. "He's not a man to be pushed around by these ragtag public interest lawyers and their six clients. It must have stuck in the craw of everyone in D.C. govern-ment, because they couldn't say they were squaring off against the NRA. They [were] squaring off against these three guys doing it on their own time, not even a law firm. One of them, Bob Levy, was not even a litigator—though he's the smartest of the three of us! It must have been incredibly galling. So I see why they would decide to bring in a top guy from O'Melveny & Myers and just *crush 'em!*"

Thus, in January 2008, D.C. changed horses. D.C.'s Attorney General Linda Singer had been replaced with Fenty's family friend and former counsel Peter Nickles. Nickles, wanting to clean house of Singer's people, fired the case's lead counsel, Alan Morrison (who himself had 20 Supreme Court cases under his belt) and recruited another one of those Supreme Court high priests Gura talked about: Walter Dellinger of superfirm O'Melveny & Myers, a former acting U.S. Solicitor General who had already been an adviser to the case for D.C.

Dellinger had to be good; this would be the *third* case he'd argue before the Supreme Court in 2008. However risky it might have been bringing someone, even someone as reputable as Dellinger, into such an argument-heavy, detailed case so late in the game, said Neily, the decision still gave Fenty cover in case of a loss. "If you lose with the highest top-shelf firms, who can fault you for it?" Neily asked. "You did what anyone else would have done: You brought in the big guys. If you lost anyway, oh well!"

Preparation for a Supreme Court appearance involves a series of practice sessions set up by your legal colleagues, known as "moot courts." Gura went through five of them, two at George Mason University, two at the Heritage Foundation, and one at Georgetown Law School. He was grilled by some of the most prominent minds in the Second Amendment debate.

Moots are invitation-only. The proceedings are secret, lest anything about litigating strategy or the counsel's likely answers sneak out to the other side. Even Chris Cox, executive director of the NRA's Institute for Legislative Action, was temporarily barred from entry to one when the woman guarding the door didn't recognize him. Other people, even those with credible-sounding claims of connection with some favored person inside, were ruthlessly excluded.

One moot attendee told me she saw Gura change an original, planned opening gambit when he realized that any statement requiring more than 15 seconds to get to the point would be lost in a flurry of justices' questions. Gillian St. Lawrence remembered the last moot at Georgetown Law School. She recalled discussion of why a long gun was not a satisfactory substitute for a handgun, given how difficult long guns could be to handle or maneuver for women or the elderly. "This was the fifth moot. Alan had become more comfortable with his answers and strategies. I think the other side underestimated our attorneys. Both my husband and I are around attorneys all the time, and if I ever wanted someone to defend me with my life on the line, my attorneys are 3 of the top 10 attorneys I have ever even heard about. They complement each other well, they are all extremely smart. Everyone knows that. But Dellinger on the other side, one of these big firm attorneys, he's kind of pompous. He thinks he can just have someone brief him on this, because D.C. couldn't get its act together. Our attorneys have lived and breathed this case. They know every detail, there's nothing they haven't read about this going back to how England's initial laws affected what we had in the U.S."

Neily remembered some of the toughest challenges from the moots: how to handle D.C.'s argument that a complete ban on handguns was fine because alternative weapons, long guns, were at least somewhat legal. Thus, any right to bear arms could still be practiced—just not with pistols. "There's analogous case law in First Amendment law," Neily said. "Like, we don't let you picket the guy's house, that's just too aggressive. But we do allow you a permit to walk up and down in front for two hours and then you gotta go. And you can send him all the letters you want. The idea is, we gave you reasonable alternatives to get your message across to this guy, although we won't let you picket his house. That seemed like it might be a really tough issue for us."

They had a great set of briefs, they had been thoroughly mooted, and the Levy lawyers knew exactly what they needed to know to sell their case. But Gura would be arguing not before some ideal abstract panel of legal minds, but before a specific group of nine justices, with their own concerns and thoughts, some of which were well-known or easily predictable.

Going in, most analysts predicted that the four conservative justices would stand up for gun rights and knock down D.C.'s gun ban. The records of Scalia, Thomas, and Alito had the more specific indicators. Scalia had publicly lamented that Americans had lost sight of the Second Amendment right and had once written that he thought the founders believed "the right of self-defense to be absolutely fundamental." Thomas, in his concurrence in the *Printz* case (overturning the enforced Brady Bill background check), wrote of "a growing body of scholarly commentary" that "indicates that the 'right to keep and bear arms' is, as the Amendment's text suggests, a personal right." Alito, before coming to the high court, had joined in a minority opinion in *United States v. Rybar* (1996) that would have overthrown the federal ban on new machine guns on commerce clause grounds. While *Rybar* wasn't about the Second Amendment, it was about guns. The Brady Center had opposed Alito's confirmation as against its interests—which it turned out to be.

A few justices could also reliably be expected, despite a general predilection to find unwritten rights in the Constitution, *not* to see this particular right that was written in plain language. And as is so often the case in modern Supreme Court jurisprudence, there was one wild card: Justice Anthony Kennedy.

In the months leading up to the hearings, the *Heller* team learned they faced another formidable opponent: the U.S. Department of Justice. Despite President Bush's stated support for the Second Amendment, and despite his first attorney general's declaration that the Second Amendment indeed protected an individual right, the Solicitor General's office, which represents the United States before the Supreme Court, filed a brief, asking it to remand the case back to the District Court rather than uphold the D.C. Circuit Court's invalidation of D.C.'s gun laws.

This request seemed to belie the principled support for the Second Amendment the administration hewed to. Vice President Dick Cheney himself signed on to an amicus brief on *Heller*'s side along with a majority of Congress (a brief arranged by the NRA). Robert Novak, in a newspaper column, explained this seeming split in the Bush administration by claiming Solicitor General Paul Clement had run off on his own with no approval from the attorney general or president. Almost everyone close to the case thinks that highly improbable and that Novak was likely fed the story to give the Bush administration political cover for the gun-rights community's outrage that its solicitor general would try to upset the glorious D.C. Circuit Court victory for the Second Amendment.

The Bush DOJ feared, they said, for the safety and health of some federal gun regulations—regulations that Ashcroft had declared were, one and all, perfectly legitimate under their new vision of the meaningful Second Amendment. The DOJ particularly feared the potential overthrow of the federal ban on the manufacture and sale of new machine guns based on Judge Silberman's declaration that a complete ban on any particular variety of weapon was illegitimate under the Second Amendment, so long as it was an "arm."

On March 18, 2008, after I visited the line waiting outside but before the hearing, I sat at the table next to the *Heller* team in the Court cafeteria. They greeted a reporter from *U.S. News and World Report*; Gura introduced his proud dad to the team. They were quiet but not somber, though their black suits made them seem so. They were not talking much about the case; they seemed to have already made their peace with whatever might await them. Kopel dryly quipped, "Welcome to Hellertown, the happiest place on Earth."

Then it was time for me to gather with the dozens of other reporters in the cramped press room. The more prominent publications and networks had their own assigned cubicles. The rest of us stood and shuffled around uncomfortably, waiting to be summoned to the courtroom. We got shuffled into our crammed seats along the left side of the courtroom right before the 10:00 a.m. start. There was barely room to place your feet on the ground between the thin wooden chairs. My view of the middle six justices was obscured by a huge pillar.

The roof is high, the room is wide, and the justices sit elevated. Even if you were not thoroughly impressed by the quality of the reasoning and intellection on display—too scattershot, with eight justices and eight agendas, sets of interests, and desires jockeying for time (Justice Thomas, as usual, said not a word during the hearing)—you could feel the gravity of grave matters on the line. The tall heavy curtains, the massive pillars, the archaic "oyez oyez" call before the justices stride in from (what I can't help think of as) backstage all set the tone.

Each side's lawyer—and U.S. Solicitor General Paul Clement as the federal government's representative—got a set amount of time to make a presentation. In theory, they must be prepared to fill it with well-considered wisdom. They know, however, with grim certainty and some small fear, that they will not really get to deliver their carefully crafted logical case, point building upon point, citation building upon citation. They won't get the chance to address and answer all the questions they can imagine a normal, educated, not obdurately opposed, interlocutor asking. No, they are certainly going to be, only seconds into their carefully prepared case, derailed by questions from the bench, questions reflecting the unique, sometimes peculiar, concerns of the individual justices.

The legal advocate for the District of Columbia, Walter Dellinger, started off with the modified "individual right" version of the Second Amendment, which, in essence, means that, no, the Second Amendment really doesn't mean a damn thing in practical terms to American citizens.

Chief Justice John Roberts prodded him on why the Framers said "the people" if they meant "the militia." Dellinger had to say, well, the terms were really congruent, so the right applied to all the people but only for a very specific militia purpose. That is, an individual right *is* inherent in the amendment. But, "it is a right to participate in the common defense and you have a right invocable in court if a federal regulation interferes with your right to train for or whatever the militia has established."

For example, Dellinger offered, a private citizen might have a cause of action under the Second Amendment if the federal government interfered with his state's right to form a militia. What the states were upset about with the national Constitution, unamended, he argued, was not that it might run roughshod over an individual right to bear arms, but rather the enormous power the Constitution gave the federal government over state militias.

If that interpretation stood, then Dick Heller's case would fall, because he did not claim his right in connection with being a member of an organized militia. Statutorily, since he was at that point 66 years old, he was not an official member of the militia, which is defined in D.C. as composed of able-bodied males between ages 18 and 45.

Dellinger was only a few minutes into his presentation when Justice Kennedy—the "swing vote"—buoyed the Levy team and sank the gun-control side by saying, "in my view [the Second Amendment] supplemented it [the militia] by saying there's a general right to bear arms quite without reference to the militia either way." He talked of how the Founding Fathers' attitudes about guns were born from a frontier experience, with worries about personal, not merely civil and political, defense involving hostile crooks, Indians, wolves, and grizzly bears. (As Halbrook told me later, with some humor, it was a shame that city boy Kennedy didn't know grizzlies weren't a problem on the frontier in colonial days, as they are native to the far western United States of today. Still, he was thrilled to detect the sign from Kennedy that he was almost certainly good for an "individual right" vote.)

Dellinger went on to deride "libertarian ideals" that he insisted were *not* in the Second Amendment, which was solely concerned, in his reading, with the "security of a free state." By then, he had to know he was on the defensive in this pivotal court hearing.

Kennedy made clear—as did Gura when his turn came up—that he didn't think the Second Amendment right to bear arms was, any more than any other right in the Constitution, not subject to regulation. Even with the historical examples from early America and England, he saw that by some of those laws, "You couldn't conceal a gun and you also couldn't carry it, but yet you had a right to have it."

Dellinger argued that the legal right to own (yet not, by the letter of the law, ever use in the home) long guns obviated any constitutional difficulties that might exist in the handgun ban. Chief Justice Roberts, straight out of the *Heller* team's playbook, made the First Amendment analogy. Roberts asked Dellinger, Would it be constitutionally acceptable for a municipality to ban books as long as newspapers— a viable substitute source of expression—were still legal?

D.C., realizing it was up against the wall, tried a strategy that seemed almost born of desperation. Dellinger openly, and in contradiction to what the District had insisted in earlier iterations of this case and in previous cases, tossed out the long gun–use regulations in hopes that, lightened of that burden, the handgun ban could continue freely on. If D.C. seemed more open to the legal use of long guns, that was an excuse to claim that the handgun regulations were reasonable. If citizens had the option of using long guns as a substitute, they were still able to practice a right to bear arms.

This was a surprise: no matter that the letter of the law clearly showed the D.C. City Council was perfectly able to articulate exceptions to the general rule about when a long gun could be loaded and used, no matter that in the 1978 *McIntosh v. Washington* case D.C. had argued the opposite. Dellinger breezily announced that, *of course*, it's "a universal or near universal rule of criminal law that there is a self-defense exception. It goes without saying. We have no argument whatsoever with the notion that you may load and have a weapon ready when you need to use it for self-defense."

Neily thought it was "so transparently obvious they were just changing their tune in order to accommodate their litigation needs. I don't think anyone in the courtroom took it seriously, and I think it damaged their credibility." D.C.'s citizens couldn't trust in a mercy that D.C. had never before shown when deciding whether they could actually use a long gun to defend themselves without risking prosecution.

I asked Gura point blank if Dellinger was lying when he told the Court that D.C. believes anyone can take off their trigger lock and use their long gun if needed for self-defense. He smiled, and answered carefully, "I'm not going to say he was lying. He might not be familiar with the record."

Dellinger's opponents weren't all that impressed with his performance. Neily told me, "I was little bit surprised he didn't have a more crisp and direct answer to some questions. I do wonder if he was as fully mooted as he might have been. I mean, you've got two other arguments in the Supreme Court, three in a month. . . . I can't imagine anybody being able to prep for three different arguments in that time.

"I also wonder if it's different for him being mooted. Moot courts, the rougher they are, the more productive. And it's one thing to be rough on Alan Gura, and another to be rough on Walter Dellinger, this icon of the Supreme Court bar. I almost wonder if anybody [during his moots] had the stature to say, 'Walter, that answer sucked. We can't tell the Supreme Court that.' Almost by virtue of being him, it must be a great answer."

Gura was, in his way, sympathetic to Dellinger's position and didn't blame *him* for any flaws in his performance. "Ultimately, it's a bad argument [D.C. was trying to make], so I don't think it really mattered who made it."

Still, Neily said, "I got the impression when Dellinger got up to give his rebuttal, I don't think even he believed the arguments. He was trying to say, hey, at least be open enough that if the idea of handguns in D.C. scares you, you can uphold this law. Maybe it's right, maybe it's wrong, but they *are* kind of scary."

Solicitor General Paul Clement, interestingly, started off with a vigorous defense of an individual rights interpretation of the Second Amendment. But his real goal was to make sure the standard of judicial review they applied to it was sufficiently loose to ensure that Silberman's alarming declaration (that once something was an "arm" it couldn't be banned) would not scuttle the federal ban on new machine guns. Clement called for an "intermediate" standard of review—one less stringent than the "strict scrutiny" standard, which requires that a law impinging on a constitutional right be narrowly tailored to meet a compelling state interest, and at the same time be the least restrictive possible means to meet that end.

What was all this about standards of review? In the angry-populist vein of Second Amendment absolutists are people who are not, in either ethical or intellectual terms, necessarily wrong but who are naive about how the political world works. To them, it is an abomination to muse over Jesuitical parsings of exactly how stringently the court should judge a law that infringes on an agreed-upon constitutional right. However, in real courts in the real world, *every* constitutional right is subject to some level of regulation. What matters is whether the government can regulate a right any time it thinks it's convenient or whether the government can only regulate a right when it's *necessary* for some *compelling* purpose. That leaves a lot of room for judicial decisionmaking, and so a three-part division was devised to decide how a court should review a law that impacts a right: on a strict, intermediate, or rational basis.

In his years of constitutional rights litigation, Neily has gotten weary of "standards of review," especially that last, loosest standard, "rational basis review." He thinks it's fraudulent for courts to say, you've got a right, "but if the government can come up with any even purely hypothetical reason for why it did what it did [to restrict that right] that's not technically insane and does not violate the known laws of the universe, they'll uphold what it did. It's incredibly unprincipled in the sense that it's a constitutional shell game. Sure, you have the right to do x, but we'll never go to bat for it. Any government lawyer sufficiently uncreative to come up with any hypothetical justification for a law is probably in the wrong line of work."

The Levy team decided to tell the Court it didn't have to figure out for sure what standard of review should apply to the Second Amendment in this particular case. If an individual right existed, they posited, D.C.'s law would fail under any conceivable standard of review. Neily noted that he and Gura disagreed on whether D.C.'s gun laws would indeed survive a "rational basis" standard. Gura thought it wouldn't, and the brief said as much.

Neily, from his IJ experience, disagreed. He thought, "No law can't pass a literal application of [the 'rational basis' standard], especially not one where they can credibly, not credibly but even plausibly, say that if we even saved *one person's life*. . . . In the end, the chief justice signaled what he wanted to do [about standards of review] and said he's uncomfortable with these different standards; why not say [D.C.'s laws constitute] a total prohibition and that just can't stand?"

Gura's performance was, obviously, a winner. In his first few seconds, though, Scalia admonished him to slow down; perhaps a first-timer's eagerness got the best of him. Gura started by demolishing D.C.'s contention that the functional ban on long guns wouldn't really be enforced, pointing out that D.C.'s representatives had never said anything like that before, despite plenty of chances, including in the earlier stages of this very case. The justices tried to get Gura to admit that certain facts—like a particularly crime-ridden city—might make it reasonable to harshly restrict guns. Scalia gently advised Gura he should answer "yes" when asked if it was unreasonable for a high-crime city to ban guns.

Gura was asked to explain the meaning of the militia reference in the preamble. He said it was to inform *one* purpose of the right of the people protected in the amendment. He angered some people in the hardcore gun-rights movement when, trying to parse *Miller*, he concluded that the weapons protected by the amendment should be ones that combined a militia purpose *and* a normal civilian purpose, since people were expected to supply weapons for the militia from the supply of weapons they typically used. Gura did not want to be pressed into arguing that machine guns should have unlimited Second Amendment protection.

He did defend ably, and at length, the idea that personal self-defense was built into weapons rights in the founding era. He granted that reasonable licensing doesn't necessarily violate the Second Amendment. And he granted that empirical considerations were meaningful in deciding what made for a reasonable gun regulation. But he stressed that the very purpose of a constitutional right is that not everything about it is up for grabs just because a legislature might think certain regulations would be "reasonable."

Gura felt a bit burned by all the Internet gun-rights activists shooting angry rhetorical bullets in the air. They were unhappy about his open admission that no one was saying the federal government couldn't keep its existing ban on new machine guns—even under the individual right, which he insisted the Second Amendment protected—because they aren't a weapon with everyday civilian use.

"Alan received lots of good advice in the moot courts," Neily remembered, "that you don't need to beat that drum to win the case, and therefore you shouldn't. Some very, very experienced and very, very smart Supreme Court litigators that Alan respects a lot advised him: Don't stake out more ground than you need to in this case. Alan did that beautifully."

"We wanted to win," Gura explained. "And you win constitutional litigation by framing issues in as narrow a manner as possible. If you ask for too much, you'll lose. You don't want to bite off more than the Court can chew at one time, consistent with the Court's own doctrine of trying not to decide cases not before it. It's a maxim of law: You only say what is needed to resolve the case and nothing more. There [are] going to be other cases where there's going to have to be balancing between individual interests and government interests in regulating, but this case is not it. It's a complete ban on people using firearms for self-defense in the home coupled with a complete ban on the most common firearm used for such purpose, and such a law will never be constitutional."

Gura thinks a lot of the radical Second Amendment advocates didn't understand the particular problems he faced. "Public advocacy is not a forum for grandstanding and making long stem-winders about the rights of individuals," he said. "It was not my place to rattle off quotations and factoids and folksy aphorisms about the Constitution. I'm getting lots of grief from machine gun owners; these people are not in touch with reality. I could not tell the justices, honestly, that I hadn't thought about machine guns. 'Gee, I don't know, maybe. . . .' That's a bunch of crap. I would have lost credibility, it would have been obviously a lie, and I'm not going to lie to the Court, and I would have lost the case.

"My job is to answer the questions I'm asked. I'm not gonna say, 'Excuse me, Justice Breyer, that's an interesting question, but I gotta tell you about something I saw on a bumper sticker somewhere.' You cannot tell the Supreme Court there is an absolute right to guns. There are no absolute rights in constitutional law. You have a right to speak about your favorite political candidate, but you are not allowed to do so at three in the morning with a sound truck in a residential neighborhood. You have all kinds of rights, and every single one of them comes with strings attached. My view of what is reasonable is very different from Sarah Brady's view of reasonable. I'd be a moron to stand up and say there are absolute rights, especially in this area."

Everyone on the *Heller* team walked away from the Supreme Court that day—especially after Kennedy's candid admission of believing the right applied beyond the militia—feeling optimistic. But hanging over their optimism was the possibility of one grim outcome. Bob Levy speculated about it before the case: what if the Court declared that, sure, the Second Amendment protects an individual right— but still felt that somehow D.C.'s laws were a reasonable response to a legitimate government need—and never mind the needs of a Shelly Parker or a Dick Heller?

6. The *Heller* Aftermath

Those to whom the Supreme Court's decision meant the world had been waiting since 1939 (at least metaphorically) for the justices to say something more authoritative about the Second Amendment than that a sawed-off shotgun didn't seem to fall under what it meant by protected arms. Everyone had longer to wait. The oral arguments were in March. Every other March case had been decided by June 23. It was the last week of decisions. *Heller* could come down any day, but it kept not being *that* day. The invaluable Scotus-Blog (the leading Supreme Court–watching news and opinion blog) made an educated guess that Scalia would write the majority opinion. He was the only justice not to have written a majority opinion in a March case. People who paid attention to the oral arguments were confident that the individual rights interpretation would win five votes. And Scalia was most likely to have an expansive reading of the rights the amendment protected. Indeed, ScotusBlog was right: Scalia did pen the majority opinion.

Scalia said everything that Levy and Gura and a generation of Second Amendment scholars had been saying. The Second Amendment protected an individual right. The prefatory clause did not restrict the operative one; that right went beyond militia service. The relevant contemporaneous debates and state constitutions supported this interpretation. The *Miller* precedent was about the type of weapon, not the people to whom the right accrued.

Oh, it was a glorious day for Second Amendment fans to read lines like these in a majority Supreme Court opinion: "The Second Amendment is naturally divided into two parts: its prefatory clause and its operative clause. The former does not limit the latter grammatically, but rather announces a purpose." "Nowhere else in the Constitution does a 'right' attributed to 'the people' refer to anything other than an individual right." "'Keep arms' was simply a common way of referring to possessing arms, for militiamen *and everyone else.*" "Putting all of these textual elements together, we find that they guarantee the individual right to possess and carry weapons in case of confrontation. This meaning is strongly confirmed by the historical background of the Second Amendment."

In addition to all those positive things for unrestricted weapon rights quoted above, Scalia also wrote:

> The Second Amendment right is not unlimited. It is not a right to keep and carry any weapon whatsoever in any manner whatsoever and for whatever purpose: For example, concealed weapons prohibitions have been upheld under the Amendment or state analogues. The Court's opinion should not be taken to cast doubt on longstanding prohibitions on the possession of firearms by felons and the mentally ill, or laws forbidding the carrying of firearms in sensitive places such as schools and government buildings, or laws imposing conditions and qualifications on the commercial sale of arms. *Miller's* holding that the sorts of weapons protected are those "in common use at the time" finds support in the historical tradition of prohibiting the carrying of dangerous and unusual weapons.

It was overall a great victory for the Second Amendment. As Joyce Malcolm had written of the English Declaration of Rights' gun provision, "though the right could be circumscribed, it had been affirmed."

Scalia's majority opinion was joined by Chief Justice Roberts and Justices Alito, Thomas, and Kennedy. Justices Stevens, Breyer, Ginsburg, and Souter dissented.

Little open emotion was evident in the august halls of the Court on the morning of June 26, 2008, when the decision was publicly announced. Various members of the original *Parker* team were there to hear how their years of effort had turned out. Clark Neily thought he detected a bit of a "dyspeptic" look on Stevens's face. Justice Stevens may well have felt upset. He authored one of two written dissents from the four justices who did not sign on to Scalia's majority opinion. A great deal of Scalia's opinion was dedicated to jousting with and debunking Stevens's arguments. Stevens thought the Second Amendment was about the militia. Full stop. He went on, of course, but added little new to the debate that had been going on, to the individual rights interpretation's advantage, in scholarly journals for decades.

Breyer also dissented, attempting to do what Levy feared the Court as a whole might do. He wrote that whether or not the Second Amendment protects an individual right, D.C.'s ban was still a reasonable reaction to the circumstances of grim urban violence—you know, the grim urban violence that increased to a dreadful degree despite the ban, and which the plaintiffs wished to be able to legally defend themselves against.

But the dissents were just that. Outside the Court the day the decision came down, winners and losers met the press. Dick Heller, especially, enjoyed his moment of glory, surrounded by autograph-seeking fans. As vonBreichenruchardt had told me during our March interview, "Dick is more than a litigant; he's an icon."

D.C. Mayor Fenty's office was initially truculent, at times refusing even to show up at City Council meetings to try to figure out what to do to adjust the District's gun laws to the Court's decision. Finally, on July 14, the mayor held a press conference to announce what the city had come up with. It was no glorious new dawning for Second Amendment liberties in the nation's capital. Indeed, Fenty admitted then and there that he knew the mildly adjusted standards would certainly get the city sued again. But he was willing to let that come, and he thought he might just win. D.C. City Council Chairman Vincent Gray admitted the whole purpose of its new gun laws was to keep as close to the old rules as possible.

You can now legally register and thus legally own handguns obtained after 1976. You can register a newly bought gun—if and when any legal source to buy such a gun appears in D.C., fully licensed as a legitimate business with both the District and the federal Bureau of Alcohol, Tobacco, Firearms and Explosives.

If you already legally own a pistol purchased out of state—even, in what is being called an "amnesty," if you have been illegally keeping a pistol in the District—you can register it now. That is, you can register it after you take it down to the cops for ballistics testing. And if you bought the pistol out of town, you can register it *after* you have it shipped to one of those (as of now nonexistent) legal dealers in the District. Oh, and you'll have to go through that whole process every year, acting Attorney General Nickles announced.

Your weapon has to be a handgun, not a "machine gun." But to D.C., a machine gun is any semiautomatic that even in theory could accept a magazine with more than 12 bullets, which pretty much covers every clip-loaded semiautomatic. That leaves revolvers and derringers apparently the only legal choices. And you can have the weapon loaded and ready to use, but only at a time of "threat of immediate harm."

Fenty made a couple of telling comments to *Washington Post* columnist Marc Fisher about how the District intended to proceed: "I am pretty confident that the people of the District of Columbia want us to err in the direction of trying to restrict guns," and "I don't think they intended that anybody who had a vague notion of a threat should have access to a gun."

Heller himself was refused the first day he went down, on July 17, and attempted to register a semiautomatic, without having the gun on him. VonBreichenruchardt made sure that the refusal was public, in front of the gathered press. Heller thought he might have to pull rank to get in front of a huge line of people trying to register, but apparently very few individuals quite trust the District's "amnesty" proposal enough to come down with previously illegal guns.

The next day, Heller brought down a .22 revolver, the original gun in the *Parker* filings, and began the process: the fingerprinting, the written test, the ballistics tests. He was told to come back with two passport photos and then let the wheels of bureaucracy grind before he could actually legally have the gun in his home. He finally got his license on August 18. Dick Heller could now legally defend himself in his home with a handgun.

Heller, while high on his victory, didn't think D.C.'s new procedures were in line with the spirit of the Supreme Court's ruling. He felt a little abandoned by his original lawyers. He and vonBreichenruchardt said, though the legal team denies it, that he was promised personal guidance through the registration process. And he was surprised to learn in the end that his semiautomatic could not be registered despite his victory.

So Heller went to the NRA and their legal star Stephen Halbrook, teamed up with one of the original *Seegars* plaintiffs, Absalom Jordan, and filed a new lawsuit on July 28. It challenges D.C.'s bizarre machine gun definition, the very limited legal window allowed to have it loaded (as Halbrook told me, basically the city said you could use the gun "if you made an appointment with a burglar"), and the police chief's discretionary power to set registration fees for weapons.

112

After the new Heller lawsuit—already known as *Heller II*—was filed, D.C. City Councilman Phil Mendelson told the *Washington Post* that the District considered the new regulations to be merely tentative. The City Council will rethink its gun laws again in the fall. (Just as this book was going to press, and in reaction to likely congressional action to overrule D.C.'s remaining gun regulations that still violated the *Heller* spirit, D.C.'s City Council did amend its regulations to finally allow its citizens to register, own, and keep loaded in the home both revolvers and semiautomatic handguns.)

The issue of standing irked the lawyers and plaintiffs from beginning to end. Despite petitioning to have the lost five reinstated as official clients, the Supreme Court said no. Dick Heller stood alone. The victory in *District of Columbia v. Heller*, in the technical legal sense, belonged to Heller, not his five comrades in lack of arms. None of the other plaintiffs would admit to feeling any lack of ownership or sense of loss in the technical defeat. They all hope that the D.C. Circuit Court will revert to a more sane standing doctrine for the vindication of constitutional rights.

Alan Gura, the sweetly vindicated champion of *Heller*, is now the lead attorney in *McDonald v. Chicago*, a suit filed by the Second Amendment Foundation challenging Chicago's handgun ban. The next frontier is the question of whether the Second Amendment will be held to apply to localities, through incorporation via the Fourteenth Amendment. This case might settle that issue.

How did the other side take the *Heller* decision? Many gun-control organizations have long maintained that they do *not* seek to completely ban weapons—and indeed, in only a handful of localities have they been. (Still, no gun-control organization has ever fought *against* such ban.) Thus, at the Brady Center when I met with legal director Dennis Henigan the day after the *Heller* oral arguments, he was already spinning his side's defeat as a victory. The most effective argument for the gun-rights lobby, Henigan posited, is "the slippery slope. That is, the Brady Bill leads to universal background checks which leads to licensing which leads to registration then eventually leads to a ban and they'll come and get your guns. So what happens when the Supreme Court takes a ban off the table and there's no horror at the end of the slope? That is a problem for the gun lobby. You read their literature: all you have to do is look at any issue of [the NRA magazine] *America's First Freedom* and see how much depends on fear of confiscation. The jackbooted thugs breaking in the door—that's why they exploited the New Orleans situation so much."

So while the NRA and other gun-rights forces see *Heller* as a vindication of what they have been fighting for for decades, Henigan and others on his side of the debate maintain the decision could clear the field in a debate too long bogged down in fears about slippery slopes. Henigan's fear about the case, he said—indeed the reason the Brady Center was so intimately involved on D.C.'s side— was that "should the Supreme Court decide that the right to have guns is broader than simply the right to have guns in relation to the militia, will it erect a substantial constitutional barrier to the gun laws we think are necessary and desirable? So the reason we have been so active in this case—and we were active from the beginning, we filed an amicus brief in the District Court, another in the Court of Appeals, and then with the Supreme Court—the reason we were so active is that we always perceived some risk that the ultimate result would be a decision that would embolden right-wing activist judges to be aggressive in striking down gun laws."

When I related Henigan's statement to various people involved in the *Heller* case on the other side, they scoffed. "Look at their literature," Gura said. "About all they say is 'guns are bad, they kill children and other living things.' Look at their website. It clearly posits gun ownership as a social evil. He can say what he wants; I like Dennis, and I've never had a negative interaction with anybody with his group, but sorry, that's a bunch of crap. His dream is dead; the idea of prohibition is dead. They need to tell their constituents to find something else to do with their lives, go be productive members of society, stop attacking our individual rights."

Whether or not Henigan was sincere, he might have a point. It is too soon to be sure, but it is possible that people who have put money and energy into fighting for gun rights might think the *Heller* decision means they've won and can retire from the legal and policy debate. However, the gun rights cause has *not* won a final victory. As is perfectly proper with a Supreme Court decision—meant to decide only the issues, facts, and cause of action directly related to the case in front of them—the decision was narrow. D.C. can't ban functional firearms. Heller gets to register his gun—his *revolver*. And he can keep it in his home for self-defense. That may be all the Court decided. That judgment says little we can consider reliable moving forward about how any other gun-control regulation will stand up under the doctrine declared in *Heller*.

Most existing gun regulation, and lots of future gun regulation, may well survive *Heller*. Although Gura grew to have little patience with the most hardcore in the gun-rights community, he told me, "To be fair, very fair to people at that end of that spectrum, there is some reasonable basis for their fears [about what *Heller* may end up *not* accomplishing]. Under the guise of common sense and reasonableness, they have seen a lot of unreasonable and nonsensical things enacted that infringe on their rights. So they are conditioned to oppose reflexively any regulation. But still, they take it too far; we don't have any absolute rights in this country, and we won't have absolute gun rights. There always will be a role for the political process. Courts won't do everything for you, and they won't get every case right."

Indeed, within two months of the *Heller* decision, a handful of lower court decisions came down in which people attempted to win on the basis of the doctrine in *Heller*. So far, all of them have failed to get any other laws or convictions overturned based on it. Nonetheless, the courts are where this particular battle was won; and that is where most of the next sorties in the war to vindicate the Second Amendment are being launched.

The NRA immediately filed four post-*Heller* lawsuits: one against a ban on handgun ownership in San Francisco public housing and three against handgun bans by various municipalities in the Chicago area. The anonymous lead plaintiff in San Francisco, a gay man who fears for his safety in a housing project, fears reprisal, because he claims to already own an illicit firearm. Most truly severe gun regulations are in localities, not states.

That latter set of lawsuits has already brought change: Morton Grove, famous for being the first nonfederal municipality to ban handguns, and which beat back a 1982 legal challenge to its gun ban in a case the Supreme Court declined to consider, announced it will repeal its handgun ban. Another Illinois town, Wilmette, which hadn't even been sued, did the same. Wilmette's Village President Chris Canning told the Associated Press, "I knew that our ordinance would not survive constitutional scrutiny." All these cases against localities will run into Fourteenth Amendment incorporation questions, the next frontier in the legal fight over the Second Amendment.

Dick Heller feels like public property now; once again a plaintiff, he's also contemplating a Libertarian Party run for D.C. Delegate to Congress, taking on speaking engagements, stressed and with little free time. He might write his own memoir. "We have what we think is a poignant story to tell to the citizenry. Dane and I started out in the basement—below grassroots level!"

He knows, though, that the principle he fought for was what was important, and the principle will continue to be important—not the man Dick Heller. He may or may not ever have to use a gun for good; he may or may not ever use a gun for evil. Neither outcome will have any bearing on the principle he fought for and vindicated. "I'm just a citizen that got upset by a violation of his rights. The citizenry simply needed somebody to raise the flag. All I did was use the system in taking this to the level it needed to go to."

He's happy to feel freer to let Heller be Heller. "Before I had to hold my breath because we didn't know if it was an individual right or not. I was supposed to be invisible and vanilla. Now, with the first decision down, I could be the worst projected image of the Second Amendment and it wouldn't matter, because now it's a matter of the fine points, and the city itself is its own worst enemy. It's really no longer about me."

Guns can kill, certainly. Cars can kill, too, and do so far more frequently. Guns can be used for frivolous or pointless pursuits. So can cars. But the principle that Heller and his lawyers and fellow plaintiffs fought to vindicate is not about death and not about frivolity. Neither is it merely *against* the state.

The principle of self-defense is *for life.* Those who philosophically believe in the necessity of a strong activist government generally do so because they can see the potential savagery of human social life. They just don't seem to want, in the case of gun control, to allow the *individual* to do anything about it.

Our legal system and our Constitution allowed some individuals to do something about D.C.'s gun laws. In the case of *Parker v. District of Columbia*, later *District of Columbia v. Heller*, a set of lawyers and plaintiffs planned, sacrificed, and acted, and they won an unprecedented victory. Because this group of people did something to preserve the right to self-defense, the rest of America will be able to as well.

Selected Bibliography

Herewith a very selected list of some of the books I found most helpful in understanding the legal and historical background of the *Heller* case and the history and practice of gun regulation in America. Not listed, but probably most important, are all the briefs filed in the case itself, which themselves give a full education on all the subjects and controversies surrounding the Second Amendment. They are all available at http://www.dcguncase.com/blog/case-filings/.

Cramer, Clayton E. *Armed America: The Story of How and Why Guns Became as American as Apple Pie*. Nashville: Nelson Current, 2006.

Davidson, Osha Gray. *Under Fire: The NRA and the Battle for Gun Control*. New York: Henry Holt, 1993.

Halbrook, Stephen P. *That Every Man Be Armed: The Evolution of a Constitutional Right*. Oakland, CA: Independent Institute, 1994.

Kleck, Gary, and Don B. Kates. *Armed: New Perspectives on Gun Control*. Amherst, NY: Prometheus Books, 2001.

Kopel, David, Stephen P. Halbrook, and Alan Korwin. *Supreme Court Gun Cases: Two Centuries of Gun Rights Revealed*. Phoenix: Bloomfield Press, 2004.

Malcolm, Joyce. *To Keep and Bear Arms: The Origins of an Anglo-American Right*. Cambridge, MA: Harvard University Press, 1994.

McClurg, Andrew J., David B. Kopel, and Brannon P. Denning, eds. *Gun Control and Gun Rights: A Reader and Guide*. New York: New York University Press, 2002.

Nisbet, Lee, ed. *The Gun Control Debate*, 2nd ed. Amherst, NY: Prometheus Books, 2001.

Snyder, Jeff. *Nation of Cowards: Essays on the Ethics of Gun Control*. St. Louis, MO: Accurate Press, 2001.

Vizzard, William J. *Shots in the Dark: The Policy, Politics, and Symbolism of Gun Control*. Lanham, MD: Rowman & Littlefield, 2000.

Williams, David C. *The Mythic Meanings of the Second Amendment: Taming Political Violence in a Constitutional Republic*. New Haven, CT: Yale University Press, 2003.

Young, David E., ed. *The Origin of the Second Amendment: A Documentary History of the Bill of Rights, 1787–1792*, 2nd ed. Ontonagon, MI: Golden Oak Books, 1995.

Table of Cases

Barron v. City of Baltimore, 32 U.S. 243 (1833)
Bliss v. Commonwealth, 12 Ky. 90 (1822)
Brown v. Board of Education, 347 U.S. 483 (1954)
City of Salina v. Blaksley, 72 Kan. 230 (1905)
Cockrum v. State, 24 Tex. 394 (1859)
District of Columbia v. Heller, 128 S. Ct. 2783 (2008)
McIntosh v. Washington, 395 A.2d 744 (1978)
Navegar v. United States, 103 F.3d 994 (1997)
Nunn v. State, 1 Ga. 243 (1846)
Parker v. District of Columbia, 478 F.3d 370 (2007)
People's Rights Organization v. Columbus, 925 F.Supp. 1254 (1996)
Presser v. Illinois, 116 U.S. 252 (1886)
Printz v. United States, 521 U.S. 898 (1997)
Seegars v. Ashcroft, 396 F.3d 1248 (2005)
Simpson v. State, 13 Tenn. 356 (1833)
United States v. Cruikshank, 92 U.S. 542 (1875)
United States v. Emerson, 270 F.3d 203 (2001)
United States v. Haney, 264 F.3d 1161 (2001)
United States v. Miller, 307 U.S. 174 (1939)
United States v. Rybar, 103 F.3d 273 (1996)

Index

Amar, Akhil Reed, 19
American Civil War, race-based gun
    regulations, 13
American Constitutional Law, 18–19
American Revolution, 5
America's First Freedom, 113–14
amnesty proposal, District of
    Columbia, 112
Aristotle, 7
*Armed America: The Story of How and
    Why Guns Became as American as
    Apple Pie,* 5, 19, 52, 74
*Arming America: The Origins of National
    Gun Culture,* 5–6
Ashcroft, John, 20, 64
assault weapons ban. *See* Violent Crime
    Control and Law Enforcement Act
automatic weapons, 50–51, 77, 111–12

background checks, 55, 113
Barron v. Baltimore, xviii
Beccaria, Cesare, 93
beheading of Charles I, King of
    England, 3
Bellesiles, Michael, 5–6
Beutler, Brian, 37
Bill of Rights Foundation, 26, 41, 67
Blackstone, William, 7, 11
Blanchard, Kenn, 28–29, 55
Bliss v. Commonwealth, 12
Bloomberg, Mayor Michael, 18
Blue Ridge Arsenal, 36
bombing of Oklahoma City federal
    building, 51, 76
Boomershoot, 80
Borinsky, Mark, 46
Bowling for Columbine, 75–76. *See also*
    Columbine shootings
Brady Bill. *See* Brady Handgun
    Violence Prevention Act
Brady Campaign to Prevent Gun
    Violence, 47–49
Brady Center, 21, 48, 55, 100, 113

Brady Handgun Violence Prevention
    Act, 49, 52, 113
    significance of, 50
Brown v. Board of Education, 59
Bureau of Alcohol, Tobacco, Firearms
    and Explosives, 51, 111

Canning, Chris, 115
Carter, Jimmy, 46
Cater, Gregg Lee, 47
Cato Institute, 25, 27, 30, 41
Centers for Disease Control and
    Prevention, evaluation of firearms
    and ammunition bans, 87
Charles I, King of England, 3, 9
Charles II, King of England, 4, 9
    restoration of British monarchy with,
    3
Cheney, Vice President Richard, 84, 100
Chicago municipalities, handgun
    ownership ban, 115
Cicero, 7
"Cincinnati Revolt," 46
citizen militia, advantages of, 9
Citizens Committee and Second
    Amendment Foundation, 46
Citizens' Committee for Right to Keep
    and Bear Arms, 45
civil rights, 47
Claremont Institute, 85
class warfare, concerns regarding, xv
classism in gun controls, 55
Clement, Paul, 100–101, 104–5
Clinton era, 48, 51
    Justice Department during, 33
clip-loaded semi-automatic weapons,
    112
Cockrum v. State, 12
Colfax Massacre, 14–15
collective rights model of Second
    Amendment, 10
colonial standing army, attitude
    toward, 9–10
Colt .45s, 28, 73
Columbine shootings, 72, 75–76

Congress on Racial Equality, 94
Connecticut colonial government, gun
    ownership requirement, 4
Cooper, Chuck, 57
Cottrol, Robert, 95
Cox, Chris, 84, 98
Cramer, Clayton, 5
Crews, Harry, 78
Cromwell era, 3
Cummings, Judge Sam, 20

Daley, Mayor Richard, 1
Davidson, Osha Grey, 47, 72
DCPPA. *See* District of Columbia
    Personal Protection Act (DCPPA)
dealers, manufacturers, importers,
    licensing for, 113
dealers in firearms, licensing for, 113
Death by Gun Control, 52
Declaration of Rights, 3
    text relating to weapons text rights
    and obligations, 2
Dellinger, Walter, 98, 102–4
Denning, Brannon P., 13
Diaz, Tom, 51
disarming of Jewish population in Nazi
    Germany, 52
discretionary powers, 112
District of Columbia Personal
    Protection Act (DCPPA), 82–83
drug dealers, 29

Edinboro, Pennsylvania, murders in, 73
elderly, 99
Emerson, Timothy, 19–21
English Civil War, 3
English Declaration of Rights of 1689,
    2–3
    gun provision, 110
English heritage of liberty, xvi

Federal Bureau of Investigation, 49
Federal Firearms Act, 43
Federalist 28, 7
Federalists, 1–2, 7
fees for registration of guns, 112
Fenty, Mayor Adrian, xv, 4, 69, 82,
    85–86, 98, 112
fiction, role of guns in, 74
Firearms Control Regulations Act, 44
Firearms Purchaser Identification Card,
    55
Fisher, Marc, 112

Flint, Michigan, shooting by child in,
    76
founding of gun-control movement,
    xviiii
Fourteenth Amendment, incorporation
    questions, 115
*Freedmen, Fourteenth Amendment, and the
    Right to Bear Arms, 1866–1876*, 14
Frye, Brian L., 15, 17
fully automatic weapons, semi
automatic weapons distinguished,
    50–51

Gage, General Thomas, 6
Gallup/*USA Today* poll, 53
Game Act, 3–4
gangs, 29
Georgetown, 36
Gore, Al, 21, 52
Gottlieb, Alan, 21
Graham, Katherine, 37
Grassley, Senator Charles, 37
Great Equalizer. *See* Colt .45s
Griffith, Judge Thomas, 69
Gun Control Act, 44, 72
    elements of, 44
The Gun Control Movement, 47
"Gun Fight," *Washington Lawyer's*
    article, 57
gun-free zones, 77
"Gun Ownership as a Risk Factor for
    Homicide in the Home," 85, 88
"Guns can kill; cars can kill too," 116
Gura, Alan
    brief writing, 94
    care in choice of judicial
    confrontation, 58
    description of, 25
    framing of issues, 107
    interpretation of Second
    Amendment, Scalia reflection, 109
    legal research scope, 61
    legal standard argument, 106
    magnitude of case preparation, 97
    opening statement, 98
    plaintiff selection, xxii, 29
    plaintiff standing to sue, 66
    procedural tactics, 63–64
    response to opponent's strategy, 104
    scope of legal decision, 115
    uphill battle to Supreme Court
    hearing, 96

Halbrook, Stephen P., 11, 14, 19, 33, 61–62, 112
Hamilton, Alexander, 7
Handgun Control Inc. *See* Brady Campaign to Prevent Gun Violence
Hanson, Tracey, 37–39
Hardy, David T., 19, 75, 94
Healy, Gene, xxii, 27, 61
Heinlein, Robert, 78
heirloom weapons, 49
Heller, Dick, xi, xiii, xvi, 26, 39–41, 65–69, 78, 112, 116
Henderson, Judge Karen, 69
Henigan, Dennis, 21, 113–14
Heritage Foundation, 94, 98
    Public Interest Legal Group, 26
honor, divisions of opinions based on, xv
Howard, Senator Jacob, 13–14
Huffman, Joe, 80
Hughes, Matt, 79–80
hunting, 44
Hurricane Katrina, attempts to disarm citizens after, 49, 114

ILA. *See* Institute for Legislative Action (ILA)
importers of firearms, licensing for, 113
incorporation questions, Fourteenth Amendment, 115
Independence Institute, 94–95
Institute for Justice, 24
Institute for Legislative Action (ILA), 46
intermediate standard of review, 105
International Action Network on Small Arms, 73

Johnson Administration, 44
Journal on Firearms and Public Policy, 93
judicial leniency, 70

Kates, Don, 19, 52, 61, 74, 85
Kellerman, Arthur, 77, 88
Kennedy, Justice Anthony, 100, 102–3
Kennedy, President John F., 44
Kennedy, Senator Edward, 47
Kennedy, Senator Robert, 44
Kerry, Senator John, 52
King, Rev. Martin Luther Jr., 44
Kleck, Gary, 19, 52, 74, 77, 87–88, 90
Kopel, David, 18, 94–95

Kristof, Nicholas, 52
Ku Klux Klan, 14–15

Lanier, Cathy, xv
LaPierre, Wayne, 51, 73
Larson, Erik, 81
Lawrence, D. H., 81
Layton, Frank, 16
Lethal Passage: How the Travels of a Single Handgun Expose the Roots of America's Gun Crisis, 81
Levy, Robert
    appeals decision, 63
    decision to bring Alan Gura into case, 25
    decision to challenge gun law on Second Amendment grounds, 23, 26–27
    effect of District of Columbia Personal Protection Act, 83
    grant of case *certiori* by Supreme Court, 82
    initiation of legal challenge based on Second Amendment, 18
    Institute for Justice attorneys, influence of, 24
    interpretation of Second Amendment, Scalia reflection, 109
    legal research scope, 61
    magnitude of case preparation, 97
    plaintiff selection, xxii, 32
    plaintiff standing to sue, 65
    prefatory textual materials in amendments, 8
    reflection on potential Supreme Court decision, 108
    timing of lawsuit, 22
liberal scholarly reappraisal of Second Amendment, 18–19
libertarians, 24, 33, 72, 116
liberty, English heritage of, xvi
locks, trigger, 34, 55, 104
Loftin, Colin, 85
long guns, 33, 35, 103–4
Lund, Nelson, 8, 57
Lyon, George, 32, 34, 51

machine guns, 48, 111
Madison, James, 1
Malcolm, Joyce, 2–5, 110
Malice, Michael, 79–80
manufacturers of firearms, licensing for, 113
martial arts, 79

McClurg, Andrew, 93
McDonald v. Chicago, 113
McIntosh v. Washington, 103
McReynolds, Justice James, 16–17
McVeigh, Timothy, 51
media, role of guns in, 74
Mellor, Chip, 24
Mendelson, Phil, D.C. City
    Councilman, 113
mentally ill, 110
Michigan Militia, 76
military officers, 94
Moore, Michael, 75–76
moot courts, 104, 107
Morrison, Alan, 98
Mossberg pump action shotgun, 34
muggings, 62, 89
Myrick, Joel, 73

Nation of Cowards, 76–77
National Academy of Sciences, 87
National Council to Control Handguns,
    47–48
National Firearms Act (NFA), xix,
    16–17, 43
  constitutionality of, 15–17
National Guard, 9
National Instant Criminal Background
    Check System, 49
National Institute of Justice report on
    ban's effect, 51
National Research Council Panel on
    Understanding and Prevention of
    Violence, 87
National Rifle Association (NRA), xxiii,
    20, 30, 33, 37, 46, 62, 73, 77, 114–15
  America's First Freedom, 113–14
  Chicago municipalities, handgun
    ownership ban, suit against, 115
  Institute for Legislative Action, 84, 98
  San Francisco public housing,
    handgun ownership ban, suit
    against, 115
Navegar v. United States, 64–65
Nazi Germany, disarming of Jewish
    population, 52
Neily, Clark, xxii, 24–27, 56–57, 83, 97,
    99, 104, 110
New England Journal of Medicine,
    homicides study, 85, 88
New Orleans, Hurricane Katrina,
    attempts to disarm citizens after,
    49, 114
New Right, rise of, 46

New York Times, 75, 78–79
Newsweek, 74
NFA. See National Firearms Act (NFA)
Nichols, James, 76
Nichols, Terry, 51, 76
Nickles, Peter, xv–xvi, 98, 111–13
nonfiction, role of guns in, 74
Novak, Robert, 100
NRA. See National Rifle Association
    (NRA)
Nunn v. State, 12

Obama, Senator Barack, 52–53
O'Connor, Justice Sandra Day, 57
O'Donnell, Rosie, 29, 54, 78
Oklahoma City federal building,
    bombing of, 51, 76
O'Melveny & Myers, 98
open carry movement, 79
Oswald, Lee Harvey, 44

Palmer, Tom, 25, 30, 32, 67, 78
Parker, Shelly, 28, 31, 78, 95, 108
Parker v. District of Columbia
  appeals decision, 63
  decision to challenge gun law on
    Second Amendment grounds, 23
  grant of certiori by Supreme Court,
    82
  gun used in filing, 112
  panel of judges, 68
  plaintiff selection, xxii, 51, 56
  plaintiff standing to sue, 65
  procedural tactics, 64
  scope of legal decision, 116
  timing of additional legal challenges,
    61
Paul, Representative Ron, 45
"The Peculiar Story of United States v.
    Miller," 15, 17
people, states, distinguished, Bill of
    Rights, 9
People's Rights Organization v. Columbus,
    59
per capita gun ownership, increase in,
    89
percentage of American households
    with guns, 79
Peters, Rebecca, 73
Pink Pistols, 94
Plesha, Adrian, 41
Point Blank: Guns and Violence in
    America, 52

political warfare, concerns regarding, xv
Polsby, Daniel, 88–89
popular media, role of guns in, 74
post–Hurricane Katrina New Orleans, attempts to disarm citizens, 49, 114
Presser v. Illinois, 15
Printz v. United States, 59
Protection of Lawful Commerce in Arms Act, 55, 58
Prothrow-Stith, Deborah, 81
Public Interest Legal Group, Heritage Foundation, 26
public opinion, 84
public safety, 86

racism in gun controls, 55
Ragon, Judge Hiram, 16
Ramsey, Charles, 67
rapists, 89
Rasmussen poll, 53
"Rational Review News," 72
Rawle, William, 11
Reagan, Ronald, 46, 49
recreational shooting accidents, 79
registration of guns, 26, 36, 49, 52, 111, 113
    fees for, 112
Reynolds, Glenn Harlan, 19
Roberts, Chief Justice John, 84, 102–3, 110
Rump Parliament, 3

safety rules for firearms, 32
Salina v. Blaksley, 10
San Francisco public housing, handgun ownership ban, 115
sawed-off shotguns, 109
Scotus-Blog, 109
Seegars v. Ashcroft, 61–64
self-defense, xvii, 77–78, 88–89, 116
self-identity, divisions of opinions based on, xv
semiautomatic weapons, 50–51, 77, 111–12
    clip-loaded, 112
    fully automatic weapons distinguished, 50–51
sexism, 36
Shields, Pete, 48–49
shotguns, 33, 36
Silberman, Judge Laurence H., 69, 83, 101, 105
Simpson, Steve, 24, 26–27

Simpson v. State, 12
Singer, Linda, 98
slavery, 29
Snyder, Jeff, 76, 80, 89
Spitzer, Robert, 78
sporting purposes, 44
St. Lawrence, Gillian, 35, 37
standards of review, 105
standing army, colonial, attitude toward, 9–10
states, people, distinguished, Bill of Rights, 9
statute of limitations, 33
Stockton, California, shooting of school children, 77
Story, Justice Joseph, 11, 86–87
Strand, James, 73
suicides, 88
Sullivan Law, 43, 54
Sulzberger, Arthur Jr., 78–79

target shooting, 44, 80
tax on weapons, 43
That Every Man Be Armed: The Evolution of a Constitutional Right, 11
Thurgood Marshall Federal Judicial Center, 40
To Keep and Bear Arms: The Origins of Anglo-American Right, 2–4
Tribe, Laurence, 18–19
trigger locks, 34, 55, 104
Tucker, St. George, 11

Under Fire, 47, 72
United States v. Cruikshank, 14–15
United States v. Emerson, xx, xxi, xxii, 19–21, 24, 26, 33, 59
United States v. Haney, 21
United States v. Miller, xix, xxi, 15–17, 21, 60, 63, 70
United States v. Rybar, 100

Van Alstyne, William, 19
Violence Policy Center, 51
Violent Crime Control and Law Enforcement Act, 50–51
Virginia colonial government, gun ownership requirement, 4
Virginia Tech, shootings at, 72
Volokh, Eugene, 8
vonBreichenruchardt, Dane, 26–27, 65, 111–12

waiting periods, 49–50
Walton, Judge Reggie, 63
Washington Post, 37, 62, 75, 112–13
Washington Times, 56, 77
Weymouth, Katharine, 37
William of Orange, 2
Williams, Mayor Anthony, 56, 67
Wilmette, Illinois, 115

Zelman, Aaron, 52

About the Author

Brian Doherty is a senior editor at *Reason* magazine and Reason.com. He is the author of the books *This Is Burning Man* and *Radicals for Capitalism: A Freewheeling History of the Modern American Libertarian Movement*, and his work has appeared in dozens of national publications, including the *Washington Post*, the *Wall Street Journal*, the *Los Angeles Times*, *Mother Jones*, *Spin*, *National Review*, the *Weekly Standard*, and the *San Francisco Chronicle*. He has appeared as a commentator and analyst on hundreds of TV and radio programs, including Fox News Channel's *O'Reilly Factor* and CNN Headline News's *Glenn Beck Show*. Doherty has served as the Warren Brookes Fellow in Environmental Journalism at the Competitive Enterprise Institute and as managing editor of the Cato Institute's *Regulation* magazine. He lives in Los Angeles.

Cato Institute

Founded in 1977, the Cato Institute is a public policy research foundation dedicated to broadening the parameters of policy debate to allow consideration of more options that are consistent with the traditional American principles of limited government, individual liberty, and peace. To that end, the Institute strives to achieve greater involvement of the intelligent, concerned lay public in questions of policy and the proper role of government.

The Institute is named for *Cato's Letters*, libertarian pamphlets that were widely read in the American Colonies in the early 18th century and played a major role in laying the philosophical foundation for the American Revolution.

Despite the achievement of the nation's Founders, today virtually no aspect of life is free from government encroachment. A pervasive intolerance for individual rights is shown by government's arbitrary intrusions into private economic transactions and its disregard for civil liberties.

To counter that trend, the Cato Institute undertakes an extensive publications program that addresses the complete spectrum of policy issues. Books, monographs, and shorter studies are commissioned to examine federal budget, Social Security, regulation, military spending, international trade, and myriad other issues. Major policy conferences are held throughout the year, from which papers are published thrice yearly in the *Cato Journal*. The Institute also publishes the quarterly magazine *Regulation*.

In order to maintain its independence, the Cato Institute accepts no government funding. Contributions are received from foundations, corporations, and individuals, and other revenue is generated from the sale of publications. The Institute is a nonprofit, tax-exempt, educational foundation under Section 501(c)3 of the Internal Revenue Code.

CATO INSTITUTE
1000 Massachusetts Ave., N.W.
Washington, D.C. 20001
www.cato.org